HIKING TRAILS I

Victoria and Vicinity

Eleventh Edition, 1993

Published by the
Vancouver Island
Trails Information Society

compiled and edited by
Susan Lawrence

Original Copyright © 1972 Outdoor Club of Victoria
Trails Information Society

Eleventh Edition Copyright © 1993 by the Vancouver Island
Trails Information Society (name change only)

First published as HIKING TRAILS, Victoria and Southern Vancouver Island in December 1972;
compiled and edited by Jane Waddell

Fifth printing February 1974
Revised, expanded and retitled November 1975
Revised February 1977
Revised April 1979
Revised and expanded October 1981
Revised and expanded January 1987
Reprinted with revision notes June 1990
Revised and expanded November 1993

Printed by Morriss Printing Company Ltd., Victoria, BC

Distributed by
Sono Nis Press
1745 Blanshard St.
Victoria, BC
V8W 2J8

Maps by A. N. Fraser Drafting Services
Cover photo by Joyce Folbigg: East Sooke Park
Illustrations by Judy Trousdell

ISBN 0-9690401-9-9

Dedication

The eleventh edition of Hiking Trails I is dedicated to Jane (Waddell) Renaud and to the founders of the original Outdoor Club of Victoria Trails Information Society.

O.C.V. members, especially Dr. Jim Fiddess and Ted Fairhurst, had long dreamed of producing a book about the trails known and used by the club. Their dreams came true in 1971 with the formation of a hard-working committee. The new editor was to be Jane Waddell, ably assisted by Bill Burroughs, John Harris, Dave Birch and Jane Toms among others. The group incorporated as a non-profit society and produced its first book in December of 1972. It proved to be an outstanding success, and by 1975 books on central and northern Vancouver Island had followed.

Jane Waddell continued as President and Editor until the time of her marriage in 1991. We are appreciative of her dedication and of the legacy that she and all the other contributors over the years leave to our Society.

In 1993, in an effort to better describe the scope of our work, and to eliminate long-standing confusion, the name of the Outdoor Club of Victoria Trails Information Society was changed to the Vancouver Island Trails Information Society. We hope that Jane and the Society both enjoy continued success under their new names.

Jane Waddell as sketched by Judy Trousdell

4

CONTENTS

⟨18⟩

●PORT RENFREW

⟨17⟩

Sombrio Beach

SOOKE

⟨16⟩

Mystic Beach

China Beach

JORDAN RIVER
●

Sandcut Creek

French Beach

10 miles

10 km

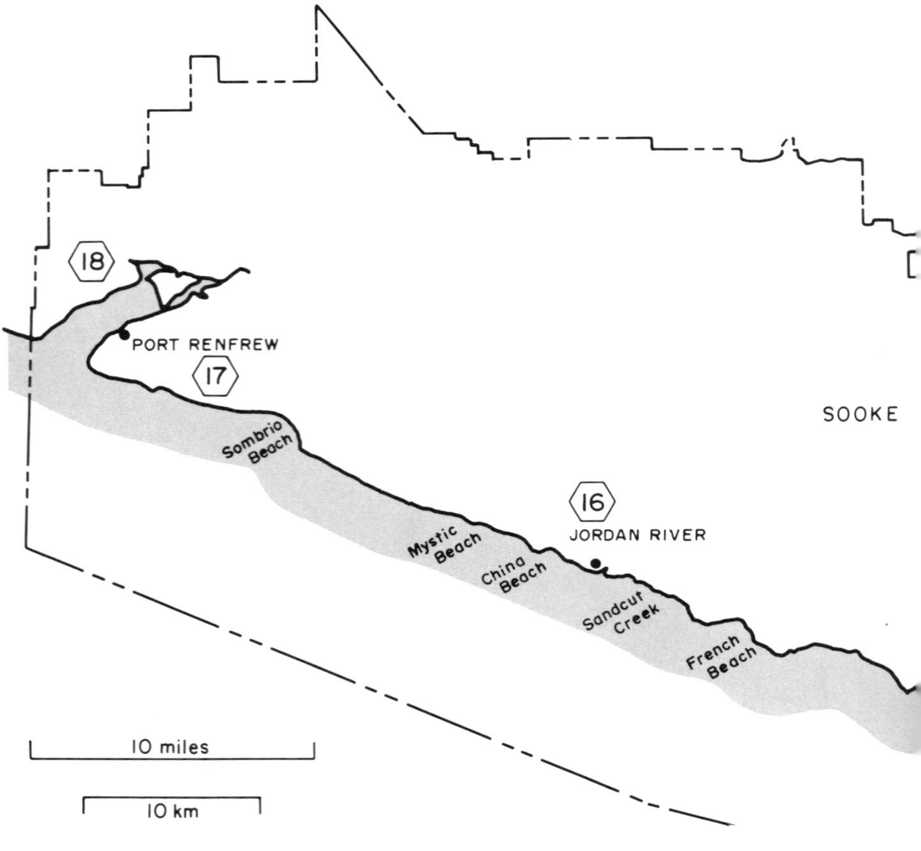

CONTENTS MAP

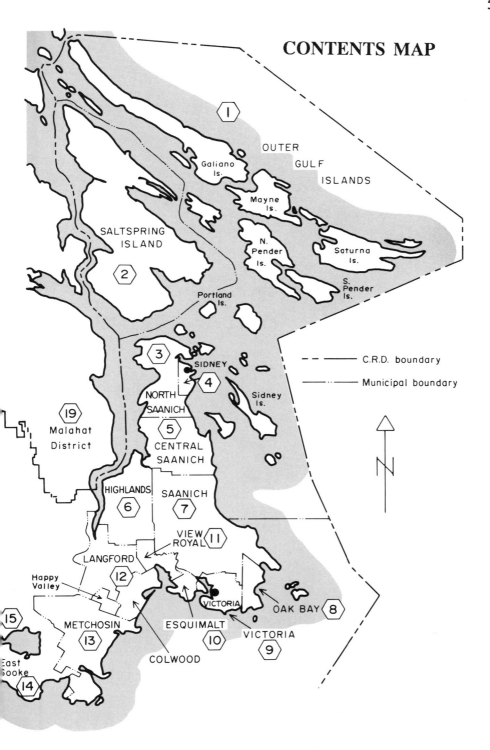

OUTER
GULF
ISLANDS

Galiano Is.

Mayne Is.

SALTSPRING ISLAND

N. Pender Is.

Saturna Is.

S. Pender Is.

Portland Is.

SIDNEY

NORTH SAANICH

Sidney Is.

– – – — C.R.D. boundary

— ·· — — Municipal boundary

Malahat District

CENTRAL SAANICH

HIGHLANDS

SAANICH

VIEW ROYAL

LANGFORD

Happy Valley

VICTORIA

OAK BAY

METCHOSIN

ESQUIMALT

VICTORIA

COLWOOD

East Sooke

N

6

CONTENTS, continued

Legend

—(17)— highway

———————— other roads

——— ——— gravel or dirt road

— — — — — trail

.... rugged trail

• • • • • • • • • • • horse trail

—+— —+— abandoned CNR right-of-way

——— – – CRD boundary

——— – ——— park boundary

——— · · ——— municipal boundary

——— · ——— DND property, Greater Victoria Water Board

——— · · · ——— other boundary (cemetery, golf course)

P ▮ parking

(P) limited parking

✳ beach access

Note that maps are not all at the same scale.

Picnic tables and toilet facilities are not shown on maps. These are termed "park facilities" and will usually be found near the main parking area.

Editor's Notes

The Concise Oxford Dictionary defines a hike as "a long tramp in the country undertaken for pleasure or exercise" and states that the etymology of the word is 'dubious.' Now, it seems odd to me, as both a hiker and a student of linguistics, that the very word 'hike' would not know where it has come from; however, with the guidance of this book, it can at least know where it is going and how to get back safely, because that is our wish for all users of this book.

Those of you who already possess an earlier edition of Hiking Trails I will notice two main changes to this expanded edition: we have reordered the existing hikes and we have added lots more.

As is apparent from the Contents Map on pages 4-5, all of the destinations described in this book, except for Spectacle Lake Park, are within the Capital Regional District (CRD), so we have pulled together the descriptions of destinations within each municipality or district within the CRD, and provided a source for further information on that area. We have ordered the areas from north to south, and then to the west. And, we have expanded your horizons within each area. On our exploratory hikes we noticed that family groups, with hikers of varying abilities, make up most of our potential readers. It was with this in mind that we added a lot of the shorter hikes (some even on pavement!) and added more information on washrooms, picnic tables, and wheelchair accessibility. The appendix giving information on bus access is new, too.

Conditions of the parks and trails that we describe in this book will constantly be changing, so we add a caution and a request: we cannot be held responsible for errors or discrepancies in this text; and, we ask that you help us to keep our books current and useful. You may write to us in care of our distributor, Sono Nis Press (address on title page). All of our books are revised regularly. In the meantime we encourage you to keep yourself updated on current conditions in these regional, provincial and municipal parks by contacting CRD Parks or BC Parks (see page 126), or the local jurisdiction (see relevant pages of this text).

As you visit the various destinations described in this volume, you may find your explorations enriched by one of the following: a current street map, one of the better bird guidebooks, and the Victoria

Natural History Society's "The Naturalist's Guide to the Victoria Region" (which has a further extensive bibliography). Should you wish to explore further afield, we can recommend our own Hiking Trails II, which covers the Gulf Islands and the southeastern portion of Vancouver Island, from Koksilah River Park to Mount Arrowsmith (revised and expanded 1993 by Richard K. Blier). Our Hiking Trails III covers central and northern Vancouver Island including Strathcona Park (revised and expanded 1992 by Jim Rutter).

The Vancouver Island Trails Information Society is a non-profit society dedicated to providing accurate information to the public about trails and parks on Vancouver Island. Any profits made from the sale of our books are donated to like-minded worthy projects.

Finally, then, let us encourage you to "take a hike": get out there and tramp about for "pleasure and exercise". See you on the trail!

Susan Lawrence
Editor, eleventh edition
September, 1993

With special thanks to the Editorial Committee: Joyce Folbigg, John W. E. Harris, Jane Toms and Ron Weir and to the other Society members: Betty Burroughs, Aldyth Hunter, Peggy Kilshaw and John Pinder-Moss.

HINTS AND CAUTIONS

Trails. While only some of the well established, better known trails are described here, they may lead to other opportunities which can be pursued by the more experienced and hardy. Most of the trails are footpaths; a few can be used by horses where permitted by park regulations. Riders should avoid disturbing the full width of trails at muddy spots. Motorized bikes are prohibited off-road in all parks.

Good clothing is essential. All these trails can be hiked in good walking shoes or even runners, but you will be better off in comfortable boots as trails can sometimes be muddy or steep in places. A small packsack is a good way to carry lunch, maps, camera, extra sweater, rainwear, swim suit, insect repellant and any essential First Aid requirements. Articles placed in a plastic garbage bag inside your packsack will remain dry in the wettest weather.

Do not litter the trails. Don't drop gum wrappers, orange peel, lunch bags or soft drink cans. Carry them out in your packsack.

Please be careful with fires, especially during dry weather. Fires are not permitted in many areas, or permits may be necessary from local fire departments. Above all, put fires thoroughly out! Clear an area free from flammable materials around your fire to a distance of at least one metre and do not establish a fire within at least three metres of any log, bush or tree. Pour water on the fire afterwards and sort through the ashes with your bare hands to be certain there are no hot spots left which could flame up again. Smoke only at rest stops . . . never when walking . . . be sure that cigarettes and matches are completely extinguished.

Map and compass. A compass and knowledge of how to use it is often useful, since one loses direction easily and even on a trail it can be difficult to tell which way to turn. To prevent your book from becoming damaged on the trail, it is a good idea to carry with you only a photocopy of the area in which you are interested.

Do not hike alone. The greatest danger is probably from slipping on loose rocks on moss-covered hillsides, or on logs. The wise hiker travels with a friend in case of an accident. A whistle is useful for communication if separated. If lost, logging roads and streams generally lead out if one follows them downhill. Cross-country scrambling is difficult, so stay on trails unless absolutely certain where you are going. Leave information on your plans, including the expected time of return, with someone who is reliable. Remember that searches in our rough terrain are difficult and expensive.

Hunting season. Be aware of the danger of being mistaken for a wild animal during hunting season and wear bright clothing. Carry a whistle or horn to warn hunters of your presence. Avoid heavily hunted areas.

Traversing private property. Ask permission. Close gates if found closed; leave them open if found open. Respect logging company signs; in this area most of their holdings are owned by them, not leased public lands. Do not damage equipment and report those you see doing so. Be considerate of your fellow hiker. Take nothing and leave nothing.

Flowers and plants. Particularly in parks where it is illegal, but in other places too, leave wild flowers where you find them. Unlike garden varieties they seldom last long when picked, and uprooted specimens rarely can be transplanted to city gardens.

Mosquitoes and other flying pests. These can be a nuisance and you may need to carry a repellant. Wasps should be avoided; they nest in the ground and in bag-like nests in trees. Poisonous plants and dangerous animals (bears) are seldom a problem. Poison oak is rare. While there are many edible plants, there are some poisonous ones. Eat wild mushrooms only if certain they are edible. The stinging nettle and devil's club may be encountered on southern Vancouver Island but contact with these is only irritating.

Do not chop "blazes" into trees. They are unsightly and lead to infection by a variety of insects and diseases. If for some reason you wish to mark a trail with plastic tape, keep use of it to a minimum as it deteriorates slowly. A more temporary marker is toilet paper, easily seen and useful in any packsack.

Hikers in Capital Region Parks should be prepared to observe a number of specific rules, subject to additional rules posted at the entrances to each park. Watch for and observe signs. Many of these rules apply in provincial parks, and most should be observed everywhere as a matter of good sense, courtesy, and conservation. The rules basically are designed to allow users and surrounding landowners quiet, peaceful enjoyment.

Most parks are open from 0700 to 2200 hours. Some parks permit "special uses" for which "park use permits" are required. These allow group activities which can be planned and organized ahead of time with the confidence that space will be available. No natural or park features or structures may be removed, damaged or polluted.

Model airplanes and alcohol are not permitted; dogs and horses are restricted. Horses are allowed only where permission is posted (i.e. "horse trail" or "bridle trail"); dogs are not allowed where signs indicate they are prohibited. Firearms (except under special permit such as for retriever trials using blank ammunition), bows and crossbows are prohibited. Particularly observe signs for boating and swimming; no swimming in posted boating areas and vice versa.

Motor vehicles may only be parked in designated areas and may only travel on roadways; vehicles left unattended over 48 hours are subject to being towed away.

Cycles are banned from trails except in specifically-designated areas.

Commercial activities and advertisements are not allowed except by permit.

Visitors to Provincial Parks should be aware of two sections of the BC Provincial Parks Regulations:

18. No person shall have a horse or other draught or riding animal in a park or recreation area except
    (a) in an area or on a trail as permitted by a sign or other device, or
    (b) as authorized by a park officer.
25. No person shall ride a cycle in a park or recreation area except
    (a) on a park road
    (b) in an area or on a trail as permitted by a sign or other device, or
    (c) as authorized by a park officer.

One final word of caution: leave your valuables at home or pack them with you. Lock the doors and trunk of your vehicle.

John W. E. Harris

⟨1⟩ THE OUTER GULF ISLANDS AREA
(see CONTENTS MAP)

Princess Margaret Provincial Marine Park (Portland Island) and **Sidney Spit Marine Provincial Park** (Sidney Island) are both covered in section ⟨4⟩: **Trails in the Sidney Area**. See pages 26 and 24.

Wallace Island Provincial Marine Park; **Mount Norman** (South Pender Island); **Mount Parke** (Mayne Island); **Bluffs Park, Bodega Ridge** and **Dionisio Point Provincial Park** (all Galiano Island), are described in another book in our series: **"Hiking Trails II: Southeastern Vancouver Island"**. The seventh edition, revised and expanded by Richard K. Blier, was published in 1993.

⟨2⟩ SALTSPRING ISLAND (see CONTENTS MAP)

Bruce Peak, Mount Maxwell Provincial Park and **Mount Erskine** are all described in **Hiking Trails II** (see above). The Victorienteers (see page 125) have produced a colour map of Ruckle Park, Saltspring Island; price: $5.00 to non-members.

⟨3⟩ NORTH SAANICH AREA

We have included only three of the parks in North Saanich: Coles Bay, Horth Hill, and John Dean, but in each case we show opportunities for you to strike off into the surrounding countryside for longer rambles. If these please you, you may wish to call in at the North Saanich Municipal Hall to pick up copies of half a dozen hand-drawn maps covering other areas such as **Deep Cove, Cloake Hill, Patricia Bay** and **Curteis Point**. These maps show the many bridle trails developed throughout the municipality.

> **North Saanich Municipal Hall**   Mail:
> 1620 Mills Road, Sidney   Box 2639, Sidney, BC
> phone 656-0781   V8L 4C1

COLES BAY REGIONAL PARK (MAP 1)

Coles Bay Park (4 ha), is about 23 km from Victoria: travel north on Highway 17 and West Saanich Road (17A). Turn left on Ardmore Drive (signposted) and left again on Inverness Road (signposted) to

14

MAP 1: COLES BAY AND ENVIRONS

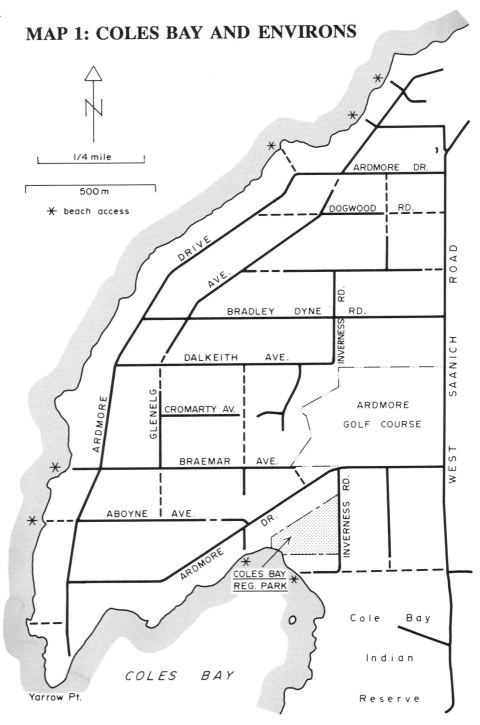

the gated park entrance. A 10-minute walk along any of the woodland trails takes you through a mixed forest of Douglas-fir, broadleaf maple and western red cedar, out to the rocky, pebble and mud beach, which is best visited at low tide. As you gaze across the bay, try to imagine life as it was for the Saanich people before European contact, when, in winter, they retreated to permanent cedar dwellings at Coles, Patricia, Saanichton and Brentwood Bays.

Washrooms (wheelchair accessible) and picnic facilities are available at the group picnic area. Trails (hilly) and beach (stairs down) are not suitable for wheelchairs.

HORTH HILL REGIONAL PARK (MAP 2)

From Victoria, travel north on Highway 17 (Pat Bay Highway) toward Swartz Bay. Just before the ferry terminal, turn left at the traffic lights onto Wain Road, then right onto Tatlow Road to the signposted, gated parking lot of Horth Hill Regional Park (31 ha)—about 30 km (a 40-minute drive). Additional parking is available at the end of Cypress Road. A grassy area near the parking lot is suitable for picnicking but most of the park is not suitable for wheelchairs. Toilets are not wheelchair accessible.

From the main parking lot the northern trail through the forest soon divides into the Lookout Trail and the steeper Ridge Trail. Both lead to fine overviews of the Saanich Peninsula and the surrounding islands, though the summit itself has no viewpoint. As you climb, notice the three forest communities represented: first, the heavily-shaded western red cedar forest, then the Douglas-fir/swordfern community at middle elevations, and finally the dry, open slopes of the Garry oak landscape near the summit. Horth Hill has wildflowers in season (look for the ladyslipper orchid) and mushrooms in the fall. As you climb the hill, look for exposed weathered outcrops of Comox Formation sandstone. Horth Hill is a cuesta or hogback hill with its smooth slope up the north side and its sharp dropoff on the south. As you explore the hilltops of the Peninsula, look for other hogback hills and evidence of glacial grooves. The deep fjord of the Saanich Inlet is testimony to the force of glacial action.

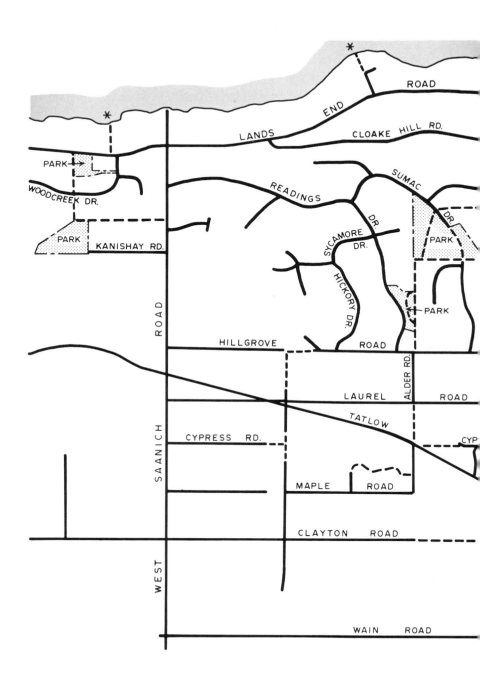

MAP 2: HORTH HILL AND ENVIRONS

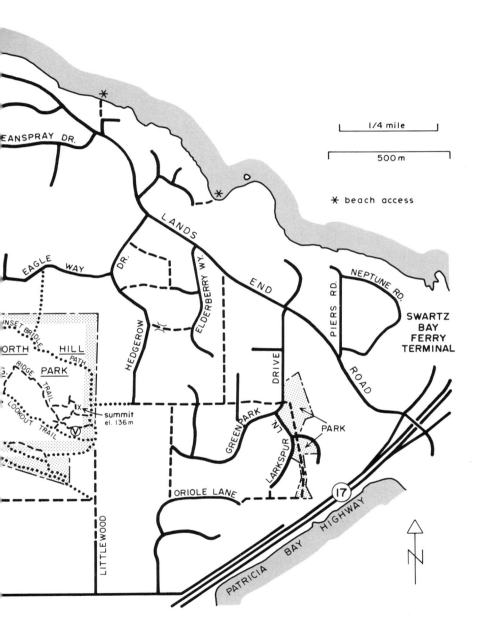

1/4 mile

500 m

* beach access

EANSPRAY DR.

LANDS

END

EAGLE WAY

DR.

ELDERBERRY WY.

HEDGEROW

NEPTUNE RD.

PIERS RD.

SWARTZ
BAY
FERRY
TERMINAL

ROAD

INSET BRIDLE

ORTH HILL

PATH

RIDGE TRAIL

PARK

LOOKOUT TRAIL

summit
el. 136 m

GREEN PARK

DRIVE

LARKSPUR LN.

PARK

ORIOLE LANE

LITTLEWOOD

17

PATRICIA BAY HIGHWAY

N

JOHN DEAN PARK (MAP 3)

From Victoria, access to John Dean Park is by Highway 17 and East Saanich Road. At **Gulf View Picnic Site** (worth a visit), turn left onto Dean Park Road which passes through Dean Park Estates and on to the parking lot. Driving time is about 40 minutes—23 km. A second point of access is off Alec Road. Travelling north from Victoria on West Saanich Road (17A), turn right on Alec Road. After 1.4 km watch for the Merrill Harrop Trail sign on the right.

The picnic area is the only area in the park that is wheelchair accessible.

Horses are permitted only on designated trails; dogs must be on a leash. See map for the following notes:

① A five-minute walk up on the gravel road (or the trail paralleling the road on the north/left side) will bring you to the federal DOT radar towers. From the viewing platform in the clearing by this site there are good views over the Gulf Islands. Look for wild flowers in season.

② Parks facilities are provided here, including a water pump. Camping and fires are not permitted. Trails north lead to a beautiful pond at the park boundary, with salamanders, frogs and water lilies. Several trails lead back to the parking lot. A circle trip around these trails takes about 45 minutes. If the hike westward up to the viewpoint over the Saanich Inlet is included, add another 20 minutes.

③ From the gravel road a trail leads down southward, which becomes the Gail Wickens Horse Trail. This crosses Thomson Place between the houses numbered 8233 and 8257 (parking here only on shoulder of road) and continues along Thomson Road unopened road right-of-way to Mount Newton Cross Road (parking space here for only one car). It is fairly steep in parts. The return trip takes about 90 minutes.

John Dean was a bachelor and an individualist with a good eye for real estate. He was considered crusty but another side of his nature was revealed after he was persuaded to let the Sidney Boy Scout Troop hold a campout on his property up on Mount Newton. He had feared vandalism, but to his amazement the Scouts—under the leadership of Skipper Freeman King—left the place cleaner than they had found it. From then on John Dean became an ardent supporter of the Boy Scout movement and showed a warm enthusiasm for the young. In 1921, at the age of 70, he donated 32 ha of his property to the province for parkland. This was the first donated Provincial Park in BC. Additions of lands donated by Barret Montfort (64 ha in 1957), Mrs. Ruth Woodward (32 ha in 1958), Sydney Pickles (7.6 ha in 1958), A. Collins (0.56 ha in 1960) and the provincial government (the balance in the late '80s) have increased the park's size to 174 ha. During the 1930s federally funded relief crews constructed what we now call Dean Park Road (originally a fire access road). Bob Boyd was the crew foreman who supervised the construction of trails and of the picnic area sited in a grove of very large trees. The steps, the stone walling and the lily pond which was formerly a swamp are all still there. This area has been described as "the most beautiful example of dry east coast Douglas-fir old-growth forest in the entire Victoria area."

John Dean died at the age of 92, having written his own epitaph seven years earlier: "It's a rotten world, artful politicians are its bane. . . ." His grave is in Ross Bay Cemetery beside a large monkey puzzle tree and is worth a visit. (See page 68.)

To link up with the Centennial Park trails and the Willow Way circuit (see pages 28-30), walk eastwards along Mount Newton X Road from Thomson Road to Saanichton School. Head south on Malcolm Road to connect with Tomlinson Road and the Hovey Road access to Centennial Park.

In 1993 this Provincial Park was offered to the Municipality of North Saanich but it was declined. By 1994 it should be transferred to another jurisdiction. In the meantime, a BC Parks brochure describing the human and natural history of the park is available. In 1984, the Friends of John Dean Park Association was formed in response to vandalism, garbage dumping and illegal plant removal. The club grew fast and, in the later '80s, built the major transit trails through the park: from Dunsmuir Lodge via the Montfort, Woodward and Harrop trails to Alec Road and the Slektain trail up the north slope.

For more information about the park, please contact BC Parks (see page 126) or the

Friends of John Dean Park
c/o 8750 Pender Park Drive
Sidney, BC V8L 3Z5
phone 656-7645

DUNSMUIR LODGE (MAP 3)

The Lodge and its grounds are the property of the University of Victoria. Public use is permitted of the Barret Montfort Trail extension between the boundary of John Dean Park and Cresswell Drive, but please be aware that you are on private property and stay on the trail. If you should wish to explore the other trails on the grounds, permission may be obtained by phone (656-3166) or at the Lodge front desk, where a sketch map is available.

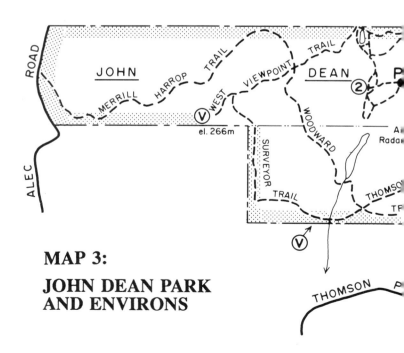

Cole Bay Indian Reserve

MAP 3:

**JOHN DEAN PARK
AND ENVIRONS**

21

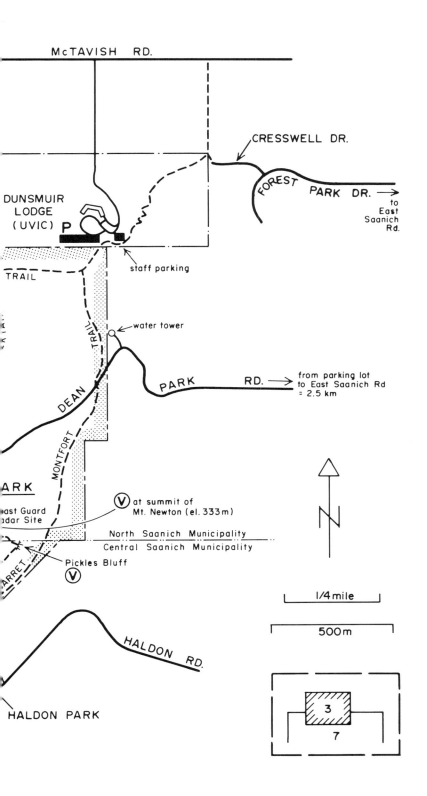

McTAVISH RD.

CRESSWELL DR.

FOREST PARK DR. →

to East Saanich Rd.

DUNSMUIR LODGE (UVIC) P

staff parking

TRAIL

water tower

DEAN PARK RD. →

from parking lot to East Saanich Rd = 2.5 km

MONTFORT TRAIL

ARK

ast Guard adar Site

V at summit of Mt. Newton (el. 333m)

North Saanich Municipality
Central Saanich Municipality

Pickles Bluff
V

HALDON RD.

HALDON PARK

N

1/4 mile

500m

3
7

⟨4⟩ SIDNEY AREA (MAP 4)

Lovely Sidney-by-the-Sea has so much to offer residents and visitors alike, so allow yourself plenty of time to be pleasantly distracted when you visit one of the three mini-hikes included here, or when you set off on the "Little Ferry" to **Sidney Island** or **Portland Island**. In particular, naturalists will appreciate the Roberts Bay federal bird sanctuary with its abundant opportunities to view marine life and other wildlife.

For more information on parks in the Sidney area please contact:

> **Town of Sidney**, 2440 Sidney Avenue
> Sidney, BC V8L 1Y7
> phone 656-1184; fax 655-4508

RESTHAVEN PARK

From the town centre, head north on Resthaven Drive to its intersection with Bowerbank Road. From the park, follow a paved promenade that hugs the shoreline out to and around the small island that was once home to Resthaven Hospital. Note that the adjacent land is private property. Wheelchair accessible.

LOCHSIDE DRIVE PROMENADE

Tulista Park, near the intersection of Weiler Avenue and Lochside Drive, is your setting-off point for this newly-constructed seaside walkway extending south to the Sidney/North Saanich border. Pick a clear day to make the most of fantastic views. The promenade itself is wheelchair accessible but access from it to the beach is by stairs. When you reach the municipal border, you are welcome to continue your walk along the beach, but be advised that the land between the beach and Lochside Drive is private property.

TSEHUM HARBOUR

All Bay

1/4 mile

500 m

N

ROAD

PARK

Boundary

RESTHAVEN

RESTHAVEN PARK

RESTHAVEN DRIVE

Roberts Bay

McDONALD

Sidney

Town

of

PATRICIA

RD.

ARDWELL AVE.

BOWERBANK

MALAVIEW AVE.

MILLS RD.

DR.

HENRY AVE.

Town

BAY

HIGHWAY

RESTHAVEN ST.

FIFTH ST.

THIRD ST.

GALARAN RD.

VICTORIA

INTERNATIONAL

AIRPORT

BEACON AVE.

of

FIRST ST.

FERRY TO SIDNEY IS & PORTLAND IS.

OCEAN AVE.

Sidney

TERMINAL ANACORTES FERRY

TULISTA PARK

CANORA RD.

WEILER AVE.

NORTHBROOK DR.

REAY

WESBROOK DR.

FROST AVE.

CREEK

17

SUMMERGATE BLVD.

PARK

LOCHSIDE DR.

North   Saanich   Municipality

Bazan Bay

MAP 4: TOWN OF SIDNEY

REAY CREEK PARK

This little park is an oasis surrounded by residential development and the traffic of the Victoria International Airport. But a true oasis it is, quiet and peaceful, with lush native vegetation and a tranquil stream which is home to salmon and cutthroat trout. Access is off Wesbrook Drive via Northbrook Drive, or where Frost Avenue deadends on both sides of the creek. As you make your way south-east toward the open parkland you will cross Summergate Boulevard, access to Summergate Village (private property). This park is not wheelchair accessible.

MAP 5: SIDNEY SPIT
PROVINCIAL MARINE PARK

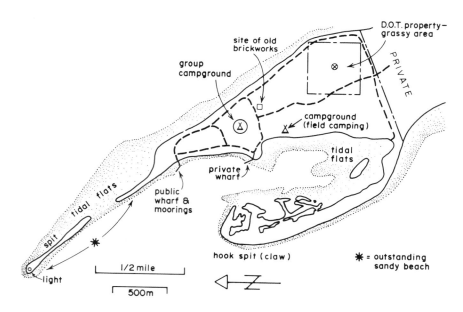

SIDNEY SPIT PROVINCIAL MARINE PARK (MAP 5)

See our Contents Map, page 5, for the location of Sidney Spit at the northern tip of Sidney Island, about 5 km off-shore from the Town of Sidney. Access is by boat or kayak or by a foot-passenger ferry, the "Little Ferry", that runs during the summer months from the foot of Beacon Avenue. In 1993 the capacity of the boat making the 25-minute trip is 40 passengers. For information on the Sidney Island Ferry phone 655-4465. On your trip over to the island watch for Rhinoceros Auklets and Heerman's Gulls.

The 400-ha park has full marine park facilities. No camping is permitted on the spit or the hook spit (claw).

At low tide one can hike for miles along the spit or claw, with year-round opportunities for the enjoyment of hikers, naturalists and birdwatchers. Fallow deer are a common sight in the open grassy fields within the park. The portion of the island south of the lagoon is privately owned.

Caution! Be careful with fires. The forest is very dry in summer and fire poses a great hazard.

Please take advantage of the recycling facilities for tin, glass and paper.

The ferry trip and the undeveloped nature of the park itself make it unsuitable for wheelchair access.

A BC Parks brochure, available from BC Parks Malahat District office (see page 126), details the human and natural history of the island and provides details about camping fees and facilities and current schedules and fares for the "Little Ferry".

PRINCESS MARGARET PROVINCIAL MARINE PARK (PORTLAND ISLAND) (MAP 6)

The whole of Portland Island is Princess Margaret Provincial Marine Park (194 ha). Currently (1993) by special arrangement with the Sidney Island ferry operator, a 40-passenger ferry can be hired, leaving from the marina at the foot of Beacon Avenue, Sidney, and landing at Royal Cove. It is about a 45-minute ferry trip. For information, phone 655-4465. There are park facilities at Princess Bay and at Royal Cove, both good seasonal anchorage for boats. Otherwise, the island is largely undeveloped. The broad trails have existed for many years, and the Youth Crew Program has constructed other trails for BC Parks. Best swimming is at the shell beach and at Princess Bay. Camping is permitted in designated areas only. As on all the Gulf Islands, be very careful with fires and build them only in the established BC Parks fire rings. Douse your campfire with water before leaving. The smaller islands around the marine park are privately owned. BC Parks (see page 126) distributes a brochure on Princess Margaret Park.

Portland Island was presented to Princess Margaret in 1958 and she graciously returned it in 1967 "for the benefit of the people of the province". The island was officially named "Portland" in 1858 after the flagship HMS Portland. Records show that in 1875 a John Palau from the Sandwich Islands (now Hawaii) pre-empted land here. This may account for the names Kanaka Bluff and Pellow Islets, as his name was spelled in a variety of ways.

In the late 1920s "one-armed Sutton", a colourful character who had served at Gallipoli, China, South America and Mexico, won a Derby Sweep Stake and bought the island, with ambitious plans. He built a stable for racing horses, planted an orchard of apple and plum trees near Princess Bay and had pens built for Chinese pheasants. The 1929 Wall Street crash wrecked his plans and though he tried to recoup his fortunes by returning to Manchuria, he forfeited Portland Island and after many vicissitudes died destitute in a Japanese prison camp in Hong Kong in 1944.

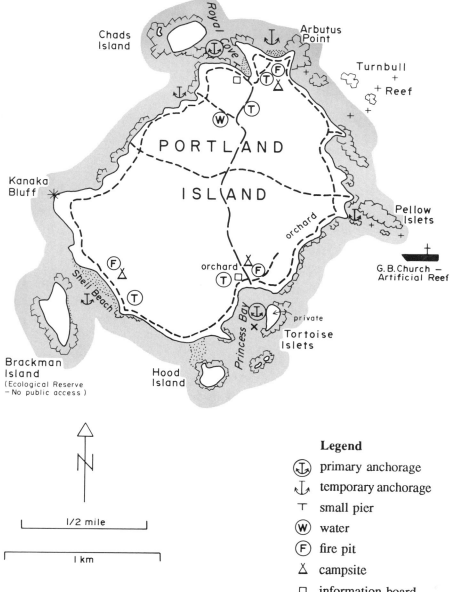

Legend

- ⚓ primary anchorage
- ⚓ temporary anchorage
- ⊤ small pier
- Ⓦ water
- Ⓕ fire pit
- △ campsite
- ☐ information board
- Ⓣ toilets
- rocks
- ✳ navigation light
- ✕ Park Host Float

MAP 6: PRINCESS MARGARET PROVINCIAL MARINE PARK (PORTLAND ISLAND)

⬡5 CENTRAL SAANICH AREA

Just walking the country roads of this rural area can be very pleasant, so don't be surprised to find that we've used some roads to link up the more popular destinations as we expand your hiking horizons.

For information on parks and trails in Central Saanich contact:

Central Saanich Municipal Hall, Recreation Dept.
1903 Mt. Newton Cross Road, Saanichton, BC V0S 1M0
phone 652-4444

JOHN DEAN PARK TO CENTENNIAL PARK (MAP 7)

John Dean Park straddles the boundary between North Saanich and Central Saanich. Descend southward from the park, following the Gail Wickens Trail through Haldon Park. Follow the Trail to the intersection of Thomson Road and Mount Newton Cross Road. Turn east along the Cross Road, then turn south on Malcolm Road near Saanichton School. You pass through farm land, then woodlands to reach the Hovey Road and Tomlinson accesses to Centennial Park.

WILLOW WAY (MAP 7)

Our map shows a pleasant 10-km circle route for cyclists, hikers and horseriders through narrow roads (where care is necessary to avoid cars) and along unopened road rights-of-way beside fences, in the flat or rolling farmlands of Central Saanich. Access from Victoria is by Highway 17, East Saanich Road and Hovey Road to Centennial Park (about 18 km—a half-hour drive) with excellent parking and parks facilities. Wheelchair access is limited to the main areas of the park.

① From Centennial Park follow the broad shoulder of Wallace Drive south across Stellys Cross Road to a footbridge due south of Stelly's Secondary School.

② Follow right-of-way south along west side of ditch switching to east side.

③ Follow Kersey Road (clearly evident at houses) to West Saanich Road.

④ Trail here is rough and grassy. Continue past greenhouses to Greig Avenue.

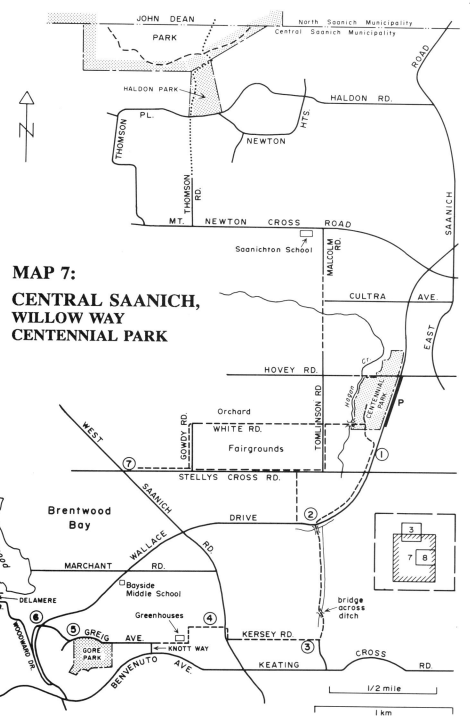

MAP 7:
CENTRAL SAANICH,
WILLOW WAY
CENTENNIAL PARK

⑤ Visit Gore Nature Park, very pretty and unspoiled. Limited parking here. At this point you can detour to Hardy Park (picnic tables) and descend along Sea Drive to the seawall promenade (public beach access, signposted) below the Port Royale development, or continue:

⑥ Via Wallace Drive and West Saanich Road go northeast, then northwest.

⑦ At Stellys Cross Road turn east to Gowdy Road and then on to White Road. The right-of-way runs along the south edge of the orchard, crosses Tomlinson Road and Hagan Creek, returning to Centennial Park.

Cautions: Be careful of private property, including fences and livestock. Keep off planted fields, especially if on horseback. Keep dogs under control. Please do not smoke, due to fire hazard. No motorcycles please.

CENTENNIAL PARK (MAP 8)

For access, see page 28 and Map 7. The Victorienteers (see page 125) have prepared a map of Centennial Park (Scale 1:3000); price: $1.00 to non-members for a photocopy.

LOCHSIDE DRIVE RIGHT-OF-WAY
(MAP 9, north section and MAP 14, south section)

The Lochside Drive right-of-way (the roadbed of the old CN Railway) roughly parallels Highway 17, passing through Central Saanich and Saanich. For a full description of the right-of-way, see page 48.

The north section of the right-of-way is almost entirely through open farmland. This makes a very pleasant walk, but note that after heavy rain there can be some muddy sections. From Lochside Park in Saanich to Highway 17 at Island View Road the distance is 5.5 km. From here the right-of-way continues north to the Saanich Historical Artifacts Society grounds (open 8:30-noon every day except Christmas Day; 8:30 am to 4 pm in June, July and August). Admission by donation. Washrooms and trails wheelchair accessible. (Please note that the right-of-way does not continue through the Society property; you must make a detour around it and the East Saanich Indian Reserve.)

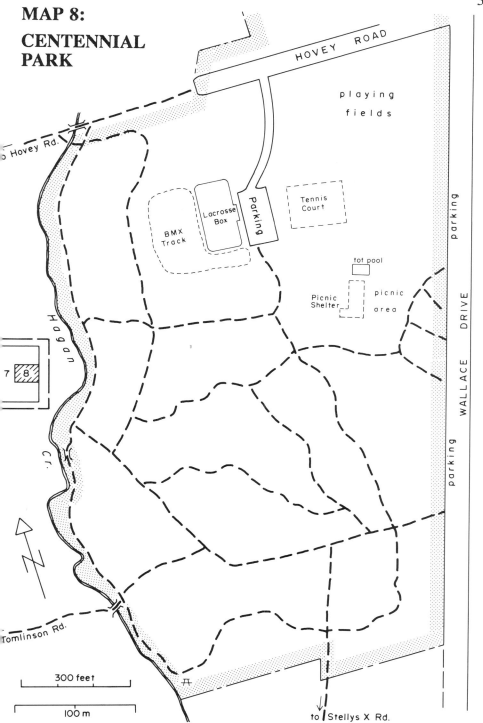

MAP 8: CENTENNIAL PARK

HOVEY ROAD

to Hovey Rd.

playing fields

BMX Track

Lacrosse Box

Parking

Tennis Court

tot pool

Picnic Shelter

picnic area

Hagan

Cr.

parking

parking

WALLACE DRIVE

7 8

Tomlinson Rd.

300 feet

100 m

to Stellys X Rd.

For more information contact:

Saanich Historical Artifacts Society
7321 Lochside Drive
R R 3 Saanichton, BC V0S 1M0
phone 652-5522

ISLAND VIEW BEACH REGIONAL PARK

From Victoria on Highway 17 travel about 16 km and turn right onto Island View Road at the traffic lights. Another 2.5 km brings you to the large CRD Parks parking lot and to the beach, a good birding area. Your route takes you through what are known as the **Martindale Flats,** an excellent observation area for wintering freshwater ducks, raptors, and the Eurasian Skylark (an introduced species once common on the Saanich Peninsula, but now increasingly rare).

Island View Beach Regional Park, now 39 ha, benefitted in 1992 from the acquisition of 10.5 ha to the south of the former boundary. Access to the park can be made along the beach at all times, or by Homathko Drive. The gate is open 7 am–10 pm, June to September. This is a Nature Appreciation Park (so all dogs must be on leash) with unique sand dunes and a berm. Please treat these natural features with great respect as the ecology is very fragile.

The toilet facilities are wheelchair accessible; trail surfaces are crushed gravel.

From a hiker's point of view this is the best and closest beach to Victoria, with a view across Haro Strait to the San Juan Islands, Sidney Spit and Mount Baker. Note that swimming is not recommended on account of strong currents.

On a minus low tide, a 10-km-one-way beach walk is possible from Island View Beach south to Mount Douglas Park with minimal rock scrambling. Note the erosion of the Cowichan Head cliffs. Another very pleasant beach walk takes you north to Cordova Spit, formed as currents carry sand and gravel from the face of Cowichan Head. Please avoid trespass on the East Saanich Indian Reserve that you pass.

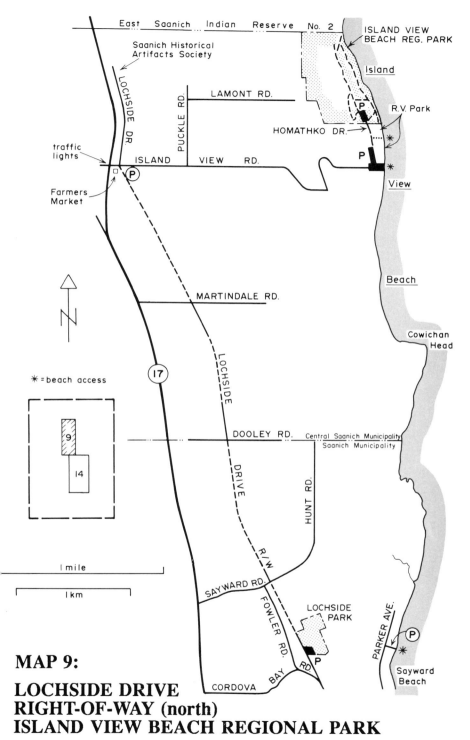

East   Saanich   Indian   Reserve   No. 2

Saanich Historical Artifacts Society

ISLAND VIEW BEACH REG. PARK

Island

LAMONT RD.

LOCHSIDE DR.

PUCKLE RD.

R.V. Park

P

HOMATHKO DR.

traffic lights

ISLAND   VIEW   RD.

P

View

Farmers Market

P

Beach

MARTINDALE RD.

LOCHSIDE

Cowichan Head

17

✳ = beach access

9

14

DOOLEY RD.

Central Saanich Municipality
Saanich Municipality

DRIVE

HUNT RD.

I mile

I km

R/W

SAYWARD RD.

FOWLER RD.

LOCHSIDE PARK

PARKER AVE.

P

P

CORDOVA   BAY   RD.

Sayward Beach

MAP 9:

**LOCHSIDE DRIVE
RIGHT-OF-WAY (north)
ISLAND VIEW BEACH REGIONAL PARK**

⟨6⟩ HIGHLANDS AREA

As we go to press, the Highlands Land District has just become an incorporated area within the Capital Regional District. This is a largely undeveloped area currently under pressure from both developers and recreationists. These volumes are revised regularly, so our next edition will reflect any changes.

In the meantime, you can visit two Regional Parks in the area: Lone Tree Hill and Mount Work.

MAP 10: LONE TREE HILL REGIONAL PARK

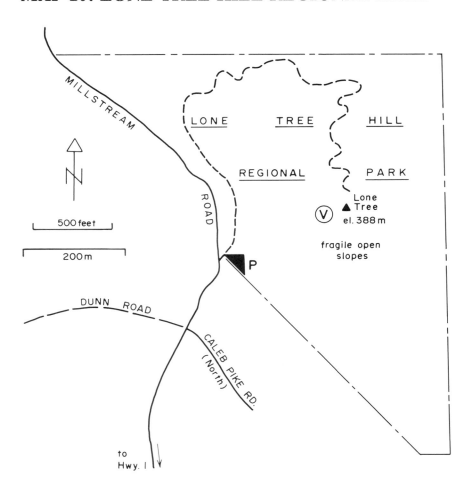

LONE TREE HILL REGIONAL PARK (MAP 10)

From Highway 1 (Trans-Canada Highway) turn north at Millstream Road. After 5.5 km take the left fork (signposted to the park) and continue on Millstream Road; it's another 3 km to the park.

The steep, rocky trail climbs steadily up to an excellent view of the Malahat, the Gowlland Range, Victoria and the Olympic Mountains. While admiring the views, watch for Bald Eagles, Red-tailed Hawks, and Turkey Vultures. The lone tree at the summit is a 200-year-old bonsai-like Douglas-fir, now a dead heritage tree. The open slopes invite one to descend over them, but please resist this temptation as the 31-ha park's ecology is very delicate. You will feel as though you are in the middle of nowhere, but actually you are subject to several restrictions: there are no bridle or bike trails and all dogs must be on a leash in this Nature Appreciation Park.

Not wheelchair accessible.

MOUNT WORK REGIONAL PARK (MAP 11)

The park (415 ha) includes the McKenzie Bight coastline, Durrance Lake and Mount Work. Access from Victoria is by Highway 17—West Saanich Road (17A)—Wallace Drive and Willis Point Road, about 45 minutes by car. Signposted parking lots give access to trails to all areas of the park—note lock-up times.

Gates are open 6 am–9 pm, April–May; 6 am–10 pm, June–September.

At the south end of the park, the Corry Road trailhead is signposted at the small parking lot on Munn Road. This can be accessed by either Prospect Lake Road and Munn Road, about 6 km beyond Francis/King Regional Park on a winding road; or from Highway 1—Millstream Road—Millstream Lake Road—Munn Road.

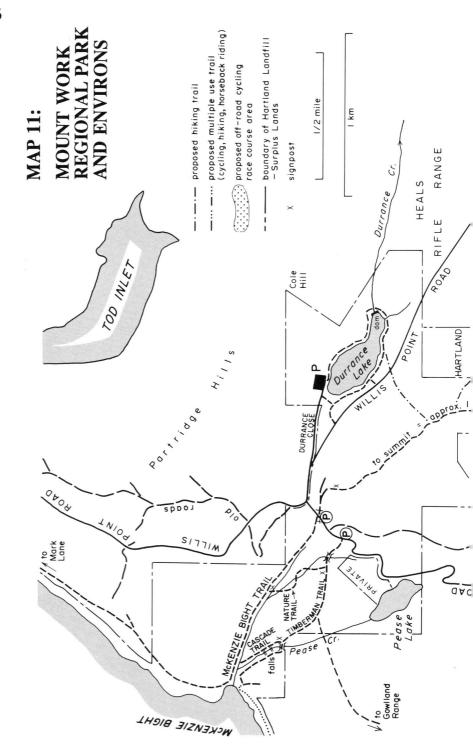

MAP 11:
MOUNT WORK
REGIONAL PARK
AND ENVIRONS

—·—·— proposed hiking trail

····—···· proposed multiple use trail
(cycling, hiking, horseback riding)

proposed off-road cycling
race course area

——— boundary of Hartland Landfill
– Surplus Lands

x signpost

1/2 mile

1 km

TOD INLET

Partridge Hills

Cole
Hill

Durrance Cr.

HEALS

RIFLE RANGE

ROAD

Durrance Lake

dam

P

DURRANCE
CLOSE

WILLIS POINT

HARTLAND

to summit approx.

WILLIS POINT ROAD

old roads

to Mark
Lane

P

P

x

PRIVATE

McKENZIE BIGHT TRAIL

NATURE TRAIL

CASCADE TRAIL

TIMBERMAN TRAIL

falls

Pease Cr.

Pease Lake

McKENZIE BIGHT

to Gowlland Range

ROAD

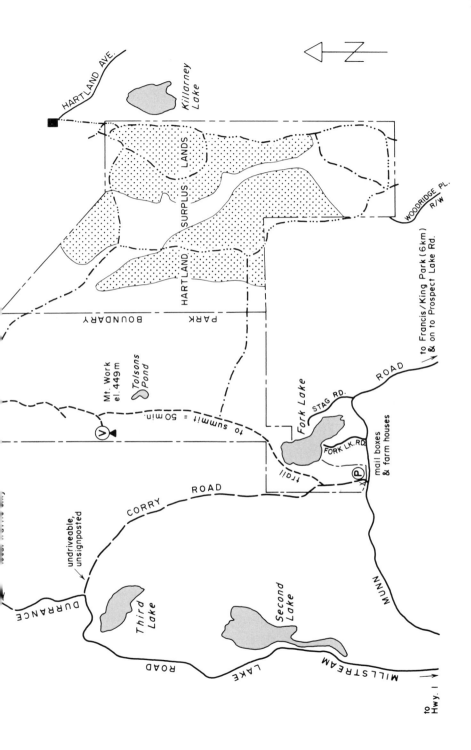

Durrance Lake is a good place to swim and a pretty trail follows around its shoreline. From the parking lot at the head of the McKenzie Bight trail to the top of Mount Work allow one hour. It is fairly steep in parts with open hiking areas and beautiful views. At the first lookout take time for views of Central Saanich and the islands in Haro Strait. From the summit overlook there are pleasant views over to Finlayson Arm and the Malahat. From the Munn Road parking lot to the top of Mount Work allow 50 minutes — good views along the way.

The McKenzie Bight trails are signposted and provide short, pleasant hikes with good picnic spots at the Bight, where harbour seals are often observed. Time down — 20 minutes. The Pease Creek waterfalls can be delightful, particularly as seen from the trail on the west side of the creek.

A 21-m parkland strip has been dedicated extending northeast from the Bight up to Mark Lane, also southwest to Elbow Point. You can follow an old road to Mark Lane. Westward from the Bight a rough trail follows the coastline to Elbow Point to a fine view up the Inlet (4 km one way).

Evidence of glacial action is all around you in this park. As you descend along the McKenzie Bight Trail, look for clay and gravel deposited in layers. Mount Work is a monadnock, or residual hill, whose hard rock — Wark gneiss — survived the grinding action, and Finlayson Arm is a glacial fjord.

If you are near the summit of Mount Work and are wondering about that shrub that resembles an arbutus tree, it's hairy manzanita, a close relative. The clusters of pink or white flowers turn into dark berries in the fall. Here's a good place to look out for Turkey Vultures soaring as they migrate in small flocks.

In the Mount Work area hikers are advised to stay on the trails as in foggy weather it is easy to become disoriented.

No camping or fires are allowed in the park, and horses and bicycles are banned.

The toilets at Durrance Lake are wheelchair accessible.

HARTLAND LANDFILL—SURPLUS LANDS (MAP 11)

As of 1993 it is proposed that this 185-ha parcel between Mount Work and the powerlines be added to Mount Work Regional Park. The area would be developed for shared use by hikers, cyclists and equestrians. For updated information please contact the CRD (see page 126).

TOD INLET / PARTRIDGE HILLS (MAP 11)

As we go to press, the future of this area is definitely "in the news". Fama Holdings Ltd. of Vancouver owns a 485-ha parcel in this area, and development is pending. If public parkland is created we will include it in our next edition.

GOWLLAND RANGE (MAP 11)

Nearly 1000 ha in this area are owned by First National Properties of Vancouver. If any new public parkland is created in this area we will include it in our next edition. For further information contact the new Highlands Municipality (see the blue pages of the Victoria phone directory) or

The Gowlland Foundation
Box 7164, Depot 4
Victoria, BC V9B 4Z3
phone 474-4124

⟨7⟩ SAANICH AREA

In 1842, James Douglas recorded the name as "Sanetch," his interpretation of the local pronunciation. In interviews with late Saanich elders, Dr. Thom Hess of the University of Victoria was able to determine that the suffix "-nutch" refers to a "behind," and that the peninsula was named for its appearance from across Saanich Inlet. The next time you stop at the Malahat lookout, imagine the Saanich Peninsula as a recumbent giant, sleeping face down, with his behind sticking up.

Saanich has over 100 parks distributed through its 107 square km. We can not describe every one for you, but you can pick up a copy of a colour brochure entitled "Discover Saanich Parks and Recreation":

Corporation of the District of Saanich
Parks and Recreation Department
770 Vernon Ave., Victoria, BC V8X 2W7
phone 386-2241

We'll cover the major parks and throw in a smattering of the more interesting short hikes, just to get you started. As you travel around Saanich, look for trail markers: posts painted with a figure of a hiker.

LOGAN PARK (not shown on our maps)

From Victoria, head north on Interurban Road. Just past the Camosun College campus turn left on Viaduct Avenue West. This narrow roller-coaster road leads you up to 6-ha Logan Park. Take along your naturalist's guidebooks for a self-guided tour of the forest and swampy areas. A new trail from the back of the park out to Hector Road gives access to country roads for longer rambles.

From the end of Viaduct Avenue you can walk along the road right-of-way to Prospect Lake Road, and from there north to **South Prospect Lake Park** (just past the golf course) for a swim or a picnic.

If you are exploring this area on foot, look for the path that follows the Elk Road right-of-way from the Interurban/Viaduct intersection (just up from the bridge) to Quayle Road. This brings you close to the entrance to the **Horticulture Centre of the Pacific,** at 505 Quayle Road (corner of Beaver Road). The Centre is open to the public every day from dawn to dusk. Office hours are 8:30-4, Monday to Friday; phone 479-6162.

FRANCIS / KING REGIONAL PARK (MAP 12)

This park is bounded approximately by Prospect Lake Road to the east and adjoins Thetis Lake Park on the west. Access: (1) from Victoria about 7 km NW via Burnside Road West, Prospect Lake Road and Munn Road; (2) follow Prospect Lake Road about 6 km generally south from its intersection with West Saanich Road just north of the Dominion Astrophysical Observatory, then right onto Munn Road.

Francis Park (43 ha) was donated by the late Thomas S. Francis in 1960 and to this has been added Freeman King Park (20 ha) named in honour of a local naturalist, the late "Skipper" Freeman King, which together with other acquisitions brings the present total to 91 ha.

Within this area can be found a great variety of terrain—rain forest, rocky ledges, woodland meadows and swamp. Trails were cut by members of the Junior Natural History Society under the leadership of Freeman King. Over the years these have been modified and renamed and are well signposted and marked with different colours. Each would take about 30 minutes to walk. Most trails lead back to the Nature House, where naturalist programs are frequently offered. In 1993, local birders were able to watch a pair of Western Tanagers raising a family in a nearby tree.

An important feature of Francis/King Regional Park is the boardwalk named for Elsie King, wife of Freeman King. This was specially constructed in 1981 so that park vistors using wheelchairs may also enjoy the park. It is complete with its own picnic table and shelter. There is also a special washroom facility for the disabled behind the Nature House.

This is a Nature Appreciation Park, so all dogs must be on leash. No horses or vehicles (including bicycles) are allowed on the trails, but there is a newly constructed bridle trail alongside Munn Road.

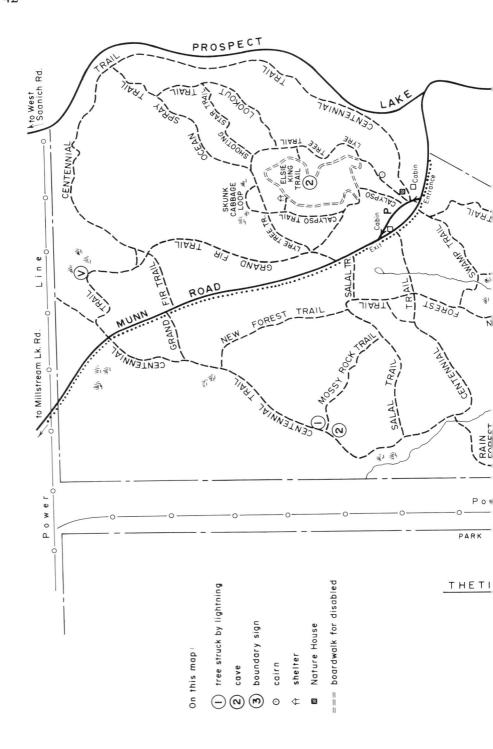

On this map:

(1) tree struck by lightning

(2) cave

(3) boundary sign

⊙ cairn

⋔ shelter

▨ Nature House

=== boardwalk for disabled

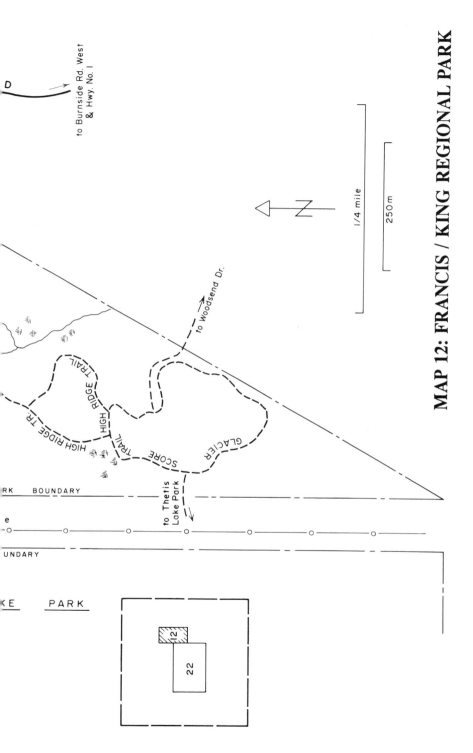

MAP 12: FRANCIS / KING REGIONAL PARK

BEAR HILL REGIONAL PARK (MAP 13)

To reach Bear Hill, travel north from Victoria on Highway 17 for about 14 km, turn left at the light at Sayward Road. Turn left on Hamsterly then right on Brookleigh Road. You can either watch for the trail to your right opposite house #541 or continue on past the boat launch and turn right on Bear Hill Road. There is limited parking on the side of the road. Look for the right-of-way beside house #5905. Other points of access are shown on Map 13.

Trails in the park are steep, rocky and sometimes slippery. They are definitely not wheelchair accessible. There are no facilities in this park, which encompasses 41 ha after new land to the east was acquired in 1993.

Bear Hill is a monadnock, a residual hill left behind by the glaciers about 15,000 years ago. Here the ice was perhaps 1,000 metres thick. Now the evidence of its passing is seen in grooves and scratches called striations. On your visit, be sure to climb every knoll and summit in order to catch every one of the views possible to all points on the compass. As you make the 30-minute climb, observe how the forest changes from Douglas-fir to arbutus, then to the dry open grass balds and Garry oak meadows. Spring wildflowers include satin flower in March, followed by blue camas, sea-blush and canary violet. The denser woods area is a good place to look for birds such as Varied Thrush and Towhee.

ELK/BEAVER LAKE REGIONAL PARK (north) (MAP 13)

Access as above. Look for the Hamsterly Beach parking lot as soon as you turn onto Brookleigh Road.

There is a beach access at Hamsterly Beach specially designed for those with disabilities. Toilets here are wheelchair accessible.

ELK/BEAVER LAKE REGIONAL PARK (south) (MAP 13)

For access to the south end of the park, follow the Pat Bay Highway (17) north for 12 km. Take the Royal Oak Drive exit, turn left onto Royal Oak Drive, then immediately turn right onto Elk Lake Drive. This park receives over a million visitors a year. It's a multi-use park enjoyed by boaters, equestrians, dog-trainers, swimmers and hikers —and Canada Geese! Horse trails are clearly identified with red horse and rider markers; hiking trails are marked with yellow markers. A walk around Elk/Beaver Lake is about 9 km. The 6 park gates are open 6 am–9 pm, April–May; 6 am–10 pm, June–September.

The Colquitz River was dammed in the late 1800s to create Victoria's first water reservoir. Filter beds were constructed in 1896 at the south end of Beaver Lake: Victoria residents were complaining that fish and tadpoles were flowing from household taps. When Victoria changed to Sooke for its water supply in 1914, the filter beds were abandoned. Though they've been filled in for years, many locals can remember playing in the abandoned cement structures as children. Elk/Beaver Lake Park was created in 1923 by the City of Victoria; in 1967 it became a regional park.

On the west side of the lake the trail often follows the bed of the old Victoria and Sidney (V & S) railroad. Opened in 1894, the rail route ran from Victoria through Royal Oak, Keating, Saanichton and on to Sidney. In its peak year, 1913, it carried 123,599 passengers and 45,282 tons of freight. Steam-driven and fired by wood, the V & S was nicknamed the "Cordwood Limited". As you walk the open, flat grade of the old rail line, try to imagine what life was like on that day in April, 1919, when Old No. 1 came steaming around the next curve on its last run, with a first class coach, combination baggage-smoker coach and flatcars in tow.

Designated parking areas and wheelchair accessible toilet buildings are located at Hamsterly and Eagle beaches and near the main parking lot at Beaver Beach.

The walk from Beaver Lake to Eagle Beach is one of the best places near Victoria for spotting cascara trees. On the opposite side of the lake, look for scat evidence of river otters. The lakes are stocked, and hold smallmouth bass, rainbow and cutthroat trout. There are more freshwater fishing days here than at any other place on Vancouver Island.

A Management Plan for the park was completed in 1992. Look for changes to the trails, parking lots and roads in the south end of the park. The Victorienteers (see page 125) have produced a colour map of the Beaver Lake area; price: $5.00 to non-members.

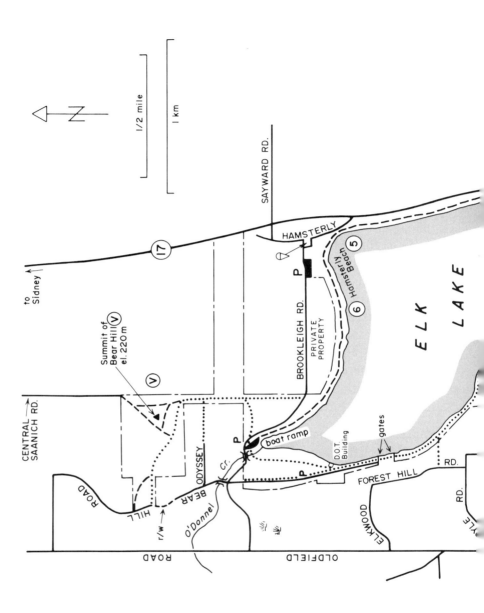

47

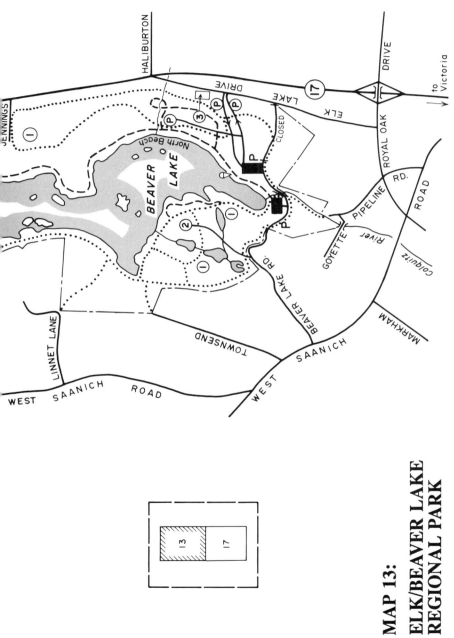

MAP 13:
ELK/BEAVER LAKE
REGIONAL PARK

LOCHSIDE DRIVE RIGHT-OF-WAY (MAPS 9, 14, 16 and 19)

The old Canadian National Railway bed can be followed from the Inner Harbour in downtown Victoria to Bazan Bay near Sidney. A good road map is the most useful tool, as north of McKenzie Avenue it is mapped and sign-posted as "Lochside Drive". It is currently partly driveable road and partly usable only by hikers, bikers and horseback riders. It is a mix of pavement through residential areas and gravel surface through farm lands and can be a most pleasant and interesting hike. It will probably eventually be the main trail on the Saanich Peninsula, connecting with the Galloping Goose extension (see page 76).

At present the Lochside Trail can be picked up in Saanich at McKenzie Avenue and Borden Street. Walk north through the Motor Vehicle Licencing parking lot to Cedar Hill Cross Road and look for Lochside Drive continuing north. It currently deadends near Blenkinsop Lake so one must detour out to Blenkinsop Road and along to Lohbrunner Road. How the trail will eventually connect around or across Blenkinsop Lake is currently being debated. Once on the other side of the lake, from Lohbrunner Road one can proceed south on Lochside through farmland to the lake. Rare and uncommon breeding species of birds to look for include Pied-billed Grebe, Green-backed Heron and Wood Duck. Wintering waterfowl species include Eurasian Widgeon and Ring-necked Duck. Heading north again, one eventually crosses Royal Oak Drive, Claremont Avenue, Cordova Bay Road, Sayward Road and Dooley Road (see Map 9). The terrain now is largely farmers' fields. North of Island View Road, plan a visit to the Saanich Historical Artifacts Society grounds (see page 30) then detour around the East Saanich Indian Reserve by diverting west to follow the Highway 17 right-of-way (visible immediately west of Lochside Drive) to Mount Newton Cross Road, then pick up Lochside Drive again to proceed northwards. At Bazan Bay the old C.N. track swung west to Patricia Bay. You may continue north on Lochside as it follows the old Victoria and Sidney Railway bed to Tulista Park in Sidney (see page 22).

SAANICH PARKS OFF THE LOCHSIDE TRAIL (MAP 14)

By its very nature, any old railway bed will tend to be flat and straight, so we offer you several opportunities to step off the Lochside Trail and explore.

When you leave **Blenkinsop Lake Park** and head north, you soon come to **Donwood Park** in the Broadmead residential development. This is just one of more than a dozen parks and trails within the subdivision. One of the best places to enter this maze is to pick up the new trail at the corner of Dalewood Lane and Chatterton Way. Follow the trail through **Shadywood Park** on out to **Emily Carr Park,** with play facilities for the children. We suggest you explore on your own, but if you feel you need a map, one is available from the Broadmead Farms office at 4599 Chatterton Way (phone 727-0101) during office hours.

When you cross Royal Oak Drive you follow paved Lochside Drive a short distance to **McMinn Park** on your right. Here you'll find tennis courts and playground equipment for the children. Just opposite McMinn Park is the entrance to **Grant Park**. This trail will test your leg muscles: it climbs to the top of Cordova Ridge. After leaving McMinn Park and continuing north, on pavement once more, look for **Doris Page Park** on your right. It leads you down to **Cordova Bay Park**, an excellent beach access.

After crossing Claremont Avenue, watch for Doumac Place on your left. It leads you into **Doumac Park**, a lushly wooded ravine.

BECKWITH PARK (MAP 14)

This park is worth a visit if you happen to be in the Quadra area. From Victoria head north on Quadra Street. Just before Quadra joins Highway 17 turn right on Beckwith Avenue. A chip trail follows the perimeter of the park and skirts two lovely ponds with Garry oak and lots of birds and other wildlife.

BOW/FELTHAM/BRODICK PARKS (MAPS 14 and 16)

On the east, these contiguous parks are accessed off their namesake streets or off Hopesmore Drive. To the west, access is off Simon Road, and on the south look for a walkway off McKenzie Avenue near the pedestrian overpass. When the decision was made not to

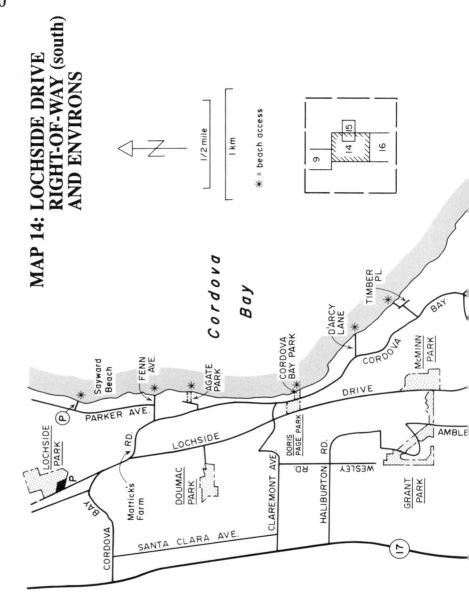

MAP 14: LOCHSIDE DRIVE
RIGHT-OF-WAY (south)
AND ENVIRONS

1/2 mile

1 km

* = beach access

9

14

15

16

Cordova Bay

Sayward Beach

FENN AVE.

AGATE PARK

PARKER AVE.

CORDOVA BAY PARK

D'ARCY LANE

TIMBER PL.

BAY

DRIVE

CORDOVA

McMINN PARK

AMBLE

LOCHSIDE PARK

P

P

RD.

LOCHSIDE

Mattick's Farm

DOUMAC PARK

DORIS PAGE PARK

CLAREMONT AVE.

HALIBURTON RD.

WESLEY RD.

GRANT PARK

CORDOVA BAY

SANTA CLARA AVE.

17

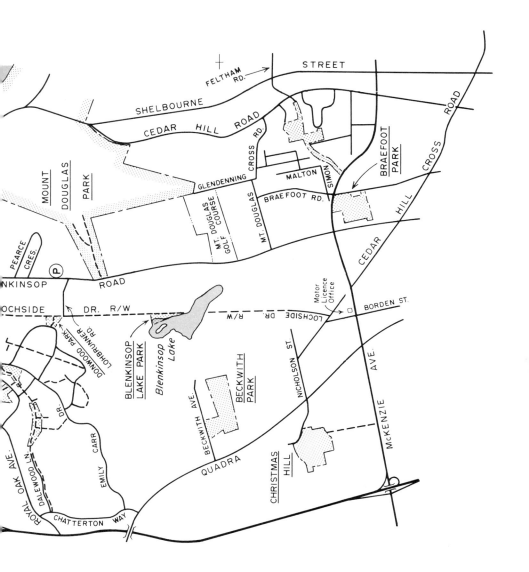

FELTHAM RD.

STREET

SHELBOURNE

CEDAR HILL ROAD

CROSS RD.

BRAEFOOT PARK

CROSS ROAD

MOUNT DOUGLAS PARK

GLENDENNING

MALTON

SIMON

BRAEFOOT RD.

MT. DOUGLAS GOLF COURSE

MT. DOUGLAS RD.

CEDAR HILL

PEARCE CRES.

Ⓟ

NKINSOP ROAD

Motor Licence Office

OCHSIDE DR. R/W

LOCHSIDE DR. R/W

BORDEN ST.

BLENKINSOP LAKE PARK

Blenkinsop Lake

LOHBRUNNER RD.

DONWOOD PARK

NICHOLSON ST.

McKENZIE AVE.

BECKWITH PARK

BECKWITH AVE.

ROYAL OAK AVE.

DALEWOOD LN.

DR.

EMILY CARR

QUADRA

CHRISTMAS HILL

CHATTERTON WAY

push Feltham Road through to McKenzie Avenue, the land was preserved as parkland, a patch of wilderness surrounded by suburban development.

Braefoot Park, with full park facilities, is just across the road from the McKenzie Avenue access, and **Mount Douglas Park** to the north is readily accessible via Malton Avenue and the Glendenning trail.

MOUNT DOUGLAS PARK (MAP 15)

This 175-ha park was originally set aside by Sir James Douglas and protected as Crown Trust since 1889. In November 1992 it was transferred to Saanich Municipality. It is 8 km north-east of Victoria at the end of Shelbourne Street. Another 1.5 km brings you to the summit parking lot and to several very fine viewpoints.

Excellent parking space and picnicking facilities are to be found at:

① from where a trail leads down to the beach. Several trails are signposted from Cordova Bay Road from which you can plan some good hiking. The Irvine Trail leads up to a viewpoint over Cordova Bay.

② No parking is allowed along Cordova Bay Road here. About 100 m beyond the quarry find the Merriman Trail (signed) and follow it to the summit—well defined and easy hiking in the lower section, but somewhat steeper with a little scrambling near the summit.

③ The Norn Trail is well defined and provides easy walking on fairly level ground. It roughly parallels Cordova Bay Road passing through tall timber; other trails lead back to ① or ③.

④ There is very limited parking space for cars along Blenkinsop Road. Between houses #4351 and #4411 find the Mercer Trail (signed) and

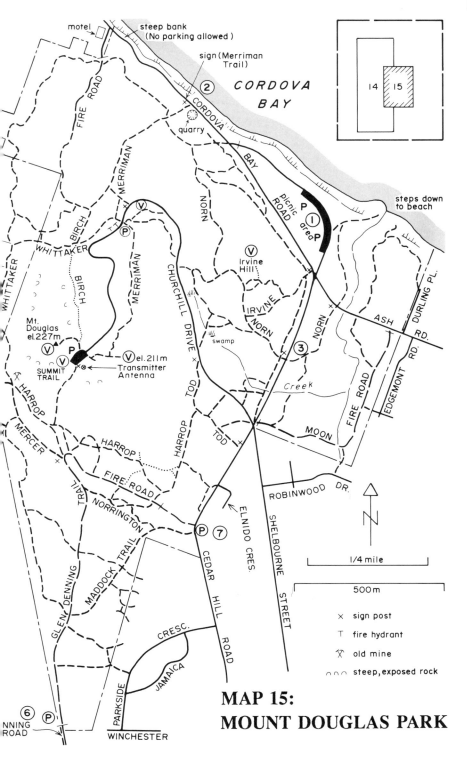

MAP 15:
MOUNT DOUGLAS PARK

motel

steep bank
(No parking allowed)

sign (Merriman Trail)

CORDOVA
BAY

FIRE ROAD

MERRIMAN

CORDOVA BAY ROAD

quarry

picnic area

P
I
P

steps down
to beach

WHITTAKER

BIRCH

MERRIMAN

NORN

V

P

T

Irvine
Hill

V

IRVINE

NORN

ASH RD.

DURLING PL.

WHITTAKER

BIRCH

CHURCHILL DRIVE

NORN

NORN

EDGEMONT RD.

Mt.
Douglas
el.227m

V
P
el.211m
V
Transmitter
Antenna

SUMMIT
TRAIL

swamp

3

Creek

FIRE ROAD

HARROP

TOD

TOD

MOON

MERCER

HARROP

FIRE ROAD

NORRINGTON

ROBINWOOD DR.

MADDOCK TRAIL

GLEN DENNING

P
7

ELNIDO CRES.

SHELBOURNE STREET

1/4 mile

500 m

CRESC.

JAMAICA

CEDAR HILL ROAD

PARKSIDE

×   sign post

T   fire hydrant

⚒   old mine

∩∩∩ steep, exposed rock

6
P

NNING
ROAD

WINCHESTER

14 15

then pick up the Munson Trail which takes you to the old mine workings. You can then climb up over a rocky ridge with Garry oak and low bush and in spring time will find lovely flowers. Or go north from the mine on the Whittaker Trail and make side trips to excellent views.

⑤ Note the blowdown here caused by a typhoon in the mid-1950s (started in Guam).

⑥ and ⑦. Very limited car parking. The lower sections of these trails offer pleasant walking through tall timber. The Summit Trail is steep and in places rocky.

No camping permitted. In the picnic area no horses are permitted at any time; dogs are allowed here from September to April only. Cycling is not permitted on any of the trails.

The **Friends of Mount Douglas** is a society formed to preserve the park in a natural state and to preserve the original park boundaries as set out by Sir James Douglas in 1889. Information is available c/o 4623 Cordova Bay Road, Victoria, BC, V8X 3V6; phone 658-5873. The Victorienteers (see page 125) have produced a coloured map of the park (scale 1:10,000); price: $5.00 to non-members.

CEDAR HILL GOLF COURSE TRAIL (MAP 16)

This walking/jogging trail is roughly in the shape of a figure eight. To begin in the middle, take Cedar Hill Road and Doncaster Drive to Derby Road and the clubhouse parking lot. A circuit of the southern loop or the northern loop would each be a little over 2 km while once around the circumference would take you 3.5 km. There are a couple of gentle hills on the southern loop, while the northern loop takes you past King's Pond with its abundant wildlife, including Red-winged Blackbirds, Virginia Rails and Ring-necked Pheasants. There are numerous benches from which to watch the golfing action. A good street map will show you other access points.

SWAN LAKE and CHRISTMAS HILL (MAP 16)

These two natural areas are managed by the Swan Lake Christmas Hill Nature Sanctuary Society (3873 Swan Lake Road, Victoria, BC, V8X 3W1; phone 479-0211). Access to the main parking lot for the Nature House at Swan Lake, if heading east, is right off McKenzie

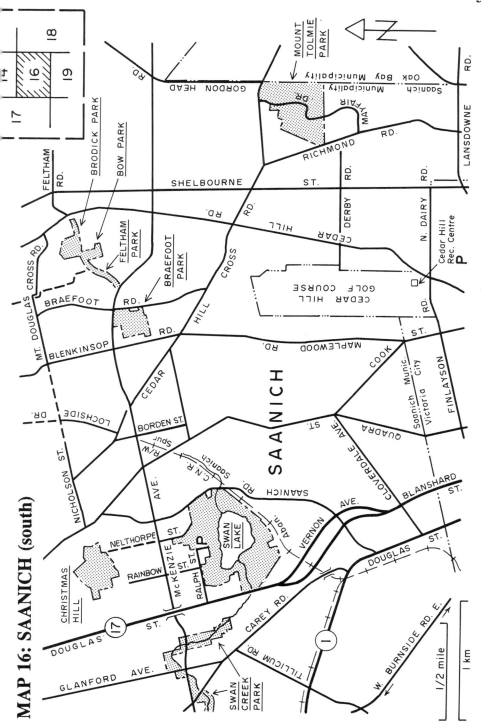

MAP 16: SAANICH (south)

CHRISTMAS HILL

SWAN CREEK PARK

GLANFORD AVE.

DOUGLAS ST.

NICHOLSON ST.

NELTHORPE ST.

RAINBOW

McKENZIE ST.

RALPH ST.

SWAN LAKE

CAREY RD.

TILLICUM RD.

W. BURNSIDE RD. E.

DOUGLAS ST.

VERNON AVE.

BLANSHARD ST.

CLOVERDALE AVE.

QUADRA ST.

Saanich Munic. Victoria City

FINLAYSON

COOK ST.

SAANICH

LOCHSIDE DR.

MT. DOUGLAS CROSS RD.

NICHOLSON ST.

CEDAR

BORDEN ST.

Spur

C.N.R.

Saanich RD.

SAANICH AVE.

MAPLEWOOD RD.

BLENKINSOP RD.

BRAEFOOT RD.

FELTHAM PARK

BRODICK PARK

BOW PARK

BRAEFOOT PARK

FELTHAM RD.

CEDAR HILL CROSS RD.

CEDAR HILL RD.

CEDAR HILL GOLF COURSE

DERBY RD.

N. DAIRY RD.

Cedar Hill Rec. Centre

P

SHELBOURNE ST.

RICHMOND RD.

LANSDOWNE RD.

MAYFAIR DR.

MOUNT TOLMIE PARK

Oak Bay Municipality

Saanich Municipality

GORDON HEAD RD.

N

1/2 mile

1 km

Avenue, along Rainbow Street, Ralph Street and Swan Lake Road. If heading west, turn left onto Nelthorpe and right onto Sevenoaks to Rainbow. The Nature House (open weekdays 8:30 am–4 pm; weekends 12–4 pm) and the toilets are wheelchair-accessible, and the old parking lot near the Nature House is reserved for handicapped parking. Cycling is not permitted and no dogs are allowed in the Sanctuary.

The Swan Lake portion of the Sanctuary features a 10-ha lake, marshland, fields and thickets, with a wood chip trail encircling the lake. Floating boardwalks, birdblinds and wharves allow visitors to get close to nature and there is a native plant garden. The 10-ha portion on the top of Christmas Hill is reached by way of Nelthorpe Street and a sign-posted trail up from McKenzie Avenue. The new Christmas Hill trails have been built to last but the surrounding area with its lichens, mosses, ferns and wildflowers remains fragile; please resist the temptation to wander off the trails. Once out on the rocky hilltop, you have unobstructed views in all directions.

THE SAANICH SPUR (MAP 16)

This section of the old CNR line known as the Saanich Spur was, in 1990, the last section to be abandoned. It extends from Highway 1 near the Town and Country Shopping Centre, past Swan Lake, across Quadra Street (where a section adjacent to Borden Mercantile is privately owned) and out to McKenzie Avenue. This section is to become part of the Galloping Goose extension (see page 76). From McKenzie Avenue north the line continues on as the Lochside trail (see page 48).

COLQUITZ RIVER LINEAR PARK (MAP 17)

Saanich Municipality, with funding from the Provincial Capital Commission, plans to develop a park and trail system from Beaver Lake to Portage Inlet. Part of this has already been developed and elaborately landscaped. The rest will be completed as opportunity arises. It is currently possible to walk from Beaver Lake to Portage Inlet on trails, unopened road rights-of-way and some roads.

A good place to start your walk is at **Quick's Bottom**, a wildlife sanctuary off Markham Street. The Victoria Natural History Society has constructed a bird-watching blind at the southern end of the marsh near the Saanich municipal nursery. Take your time; more than one birder has added to a life list here. The bottom land is part of the original Quick family farm where William and Esther (nee Carmichael) Quick raised their family and tended the first herd of registered Jersey cattle on Vancouver Island. As you leave the park at Wilkinson Road, detour south a short distance to pick up a rough trail off Lindsay Street (hints: one trail begins under a grand fir ("balsam") tree beneath the street light, and another begins over three large, rough boulders.) Be prepared for thistles, blackberries and mud, even in summer. You must also cross a small creek before coming out to the Colquitz River and the trail coming in from **Brydon Park**. It is sometimes possible to cross the Colquitz River here on stepping-stones to join a good trail leading out to Mann Avenue (signposted). Or, use the Casa Linda trail. Once out onto Mann Avenue good trails lead to **Copley Park** or out to other streets. Heading south from Copley Park, cross Carey Road and follow Grange Road to Roy Road. On the other side of Roy Road you are entering the Panama Flats area. There is still no bridge at the south end of the flats, but a sturdy wooden plank serves the purpose for now. If necessary, make a detour out onto Interurban Road just north of **Hyacinth Park**. Once you have reached Hyacinth Park you are in the developed part of the park and can head south to the Tillicum Mall and **Cuthbert Holmes Park** on good trails, most of them wheelchair accessible. This section of the trail parallels Interurban Road, originally the railbed for the BC Electric Railway's line out to Deep Cove. There are several access points off Interurban. On the other side of the trail, access is possible on a footbridge from Nora Place, off Rolston Crescent, or from the Pacific Forestry Centre.

SWAN CREEK TRAIL (MAP 17)

From the **Colquitz River Park** at **Hyacinth Park** you can pick up a trail just off Marigold Road that will take you along Swan Creek all the way to the allotment gardens off Ralph Street. This does involve a short section along heavily-travelled McKenzie Avenue, and you arrive to find that the **Swan Lake Christmas Hill Nature Sanctuary** is just on the other side of busy Douglas Street.

MAP 17: COLQUITZ RIVER LINEAR PARK

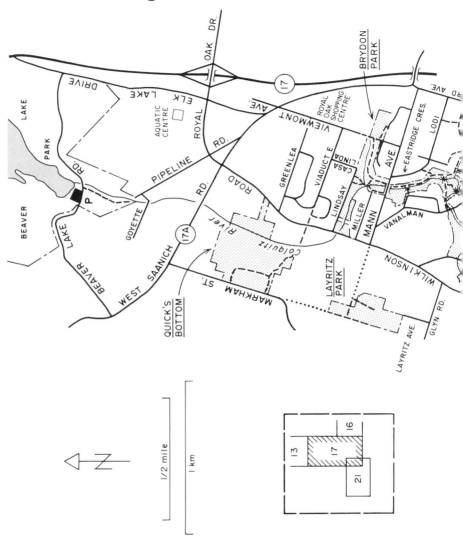

CUTHBERT HOLMES PARK (MAP 17)

Vehicle access is off Admirals Road near Highway 1; pedestrian access is off Dysart Road, from behind the Pearkes Arena, or from the south end of the Colquitz River Linear Park. Asphalt paths and chip trails offer ready access to this forested 27-ha nature park, home to 55 bird species including Great Blue Herons.

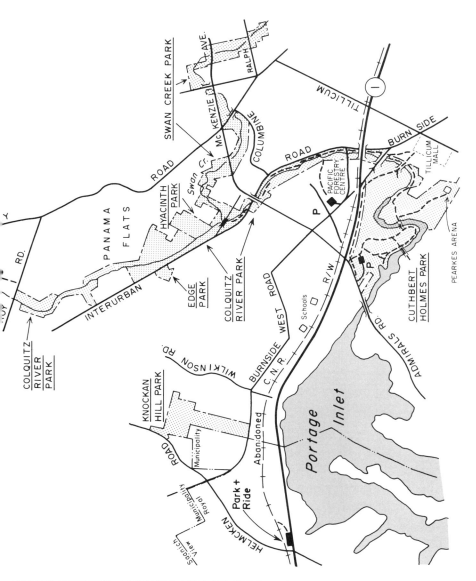

GALLOPING GOOSE EXTENSION (MAPS 17, 19 and 21)

The old CNR right-of-way runs 9.5 km from downtown Victoria, through Saanich (roughly paralleling the Trans-Canada Highway), and on to View Royal, where, from Atkins on, it has been developed as the Galloping Goose Regional Trail. Another section, the 2-km Saanich spur, runs from the Town and Country Shopping Centre area out to McKenzie Avenue (see page 56). In July, 1993, it was announced that these sections of the right-of-way will be leased from the Highways Ministry and developed as an extension of the Galloping Goose Trail. The recreational lease will provide for bicycle and pedestrian use while preserving the route for future transportation needs. We show it on our maps as Abandoned C.N.R. R/W. Caution: at present there is no crosswalk where the right-of-way crosses Highway 1 near the Town and Country Shopping Centre.

KNOCKAN HILL PARK (MAP 17)

If you are travelling along the CNR right-of-way between Atkins and the Town and Country Shopping Centre (the Galloping Goose Extension), an interesting side trip can be made by turning up Wilkinson Road to Burnside Road and heading west a short distance to the entrance to Knockan Hill Park. You soon come across a stucco house from the thirties. Known as Stranton Lodge, and designed by Hubert Savage in the English Arts and Crafts Style, it is the former home of Thomas and Maude Hall. The building and grounds have been designated a heritage site, and restoration is being undertaken by the Saanich Heritage Foundation. Past Stranton Lodge ("Hall Cottage") the trail climbs to an open rocky summit affording good views to the north and east. Access is also possible from the end of Mildred Street and off Helmcken Road near the intersection of Holland Avenue. Cycling is prohibited.

"Knockan" may be derived from the Songhees word "nga'k'un'," meaning "coiled up (like a rope)". Possibly it comes from the Gaelic "cnocan", meaning "small hill"; the name was established by the time of Walter C. Grant's survey in 1852. The **Friends of Knockan Hill Park Society** was formed in 1990 to preserve the flora and fauna and the natural character of the park. For information or a descriptive brochure contact the society c/o 81 High Street, Victoria, BC V8Z 5C8.

GORGE WATERWAY PARK and GORGE PARK (MAP 20)

Gorge Waterway Park is bounded by Admirals Road, Gorge Road West, Gorge View Drive and The Gorge Waters, but there are no bounds to the number of smiles you'll meet from people of all ages as you make your way along the asphalt path. From babies in buggies to seniors with walkers, everyone enjoys the Gorge Waterway. You could combine your walk with a visit to the **Craigflower Farmhouse and School**, two historical sites nearby on Admirals Road. Less well known is Gorge Park, bounded by Tillicum Road, Gorge Road West, the foot of Millgrove and the waters of The Gorge. Just across the Tillicum Road bridge is **Kinsmen Gorge Park** in Esquimalt. Under the bridge, you may observe the reversing falls as the tide changes. The waterway was earlier called "Camosack" or "Camosun" and gave its name to the site of the fur-trading post that would later become Victoria. "Camossung" was from the Songhees legend of a little girl who, along with her grandfather, was turned into a stone at the site of the falls. "Camosun" was proposed as the name of what was to be called the Empress Hotel; later it was chosen for Victoria's Camosun College.

GLENCOE COVE

This area, not shown on any of our maps, is a 15-ha parcel near Vantreight Drive and Ferndale Road. Access at present is off Shore Way off Pauls Terrace. The owners, Stanrick Group Inc., propose developing the land for housing. A local group, the **Friends of Glencoe Cove** (phone 477-5177 or 721-0169), has been formed in support of developing the property as a waterfront park. Features of the area include: aboriginal burial cairns, shell middens, rare plants, Garry oaks, a cormorant rookery and other animal and bird life. There are two small, secluded beaches, a pocket cove, and the potential for a trail system. If any part of this property is developed as public parkland, we will include it in our next edition. In the meantime, current information is available from the Saanich planning department.

UNIVERSITY OF VICTORIA LANDS (MAP 18)

The UVic campus straddles the Saanich/Oak Bay municipal border. Surrounding the campus is a walking/jogging trail known as the **"Chip Trip"**. A circuit will lead you through the **University Gardens**, which include an outstanding rhododendron collection, and a detour will take you across Cedar Hill Cross Road (take care in crossing!) to the **Henderson Recreation Centre** in Oak Bay (see page 64). A 4.6-ha parcel of land adjacent to the east side of the campus was acquired in 1993 to become an ecological protection area. This forested ravine, an idyllic spot still echoing with legends, is known as **Mystic Vale** and may be reached from Haro Road or the south end of Hobbs Street.

The Victorienteers (see page 125) have produced a map of the university area (scale 1:7500); price $1.00 to non-members for a photocopy.

MOUNT TOLMIE (MAPS 16 and 18)

The University grounds are a good setting-off point for hikes up Mount Tolmie. Look on the map for the intersection of Gordon Head Road, Mayfair Drive and Cedar Hill Cross Road for just one place to start. The 360-degree view from the summit is worth every bit of effort! Cycling is banned from the park trails. The Victorienteers (see page 125) have produced a colour map of the park; price: $5.00 to non-members.

THE TEN MILE POINT AREA (MAP 18)

Saanich has provided many signposted walkways throughout the area for the convenience and pleasure of the residents. A good street map will point them out to you. As you explore, don't overlook these highlights: at the east end of the Arbutus Road loop look beside house #2809 for a path with rock retaining walls and a metal handrail. It leads to a wooden viewing platform on part of **Phyllis Park**. It's a great place to take a lunch. Nearby, beside house #2801, an emergency road (pedestrians only) leads you to the end of Phyllis Street and the start of a trail that leads down to great views out over the water (though, alas, no easy beach access). Don't overlook **Konukson Park**, on Sea Point Drive. Take your time to observe how the range of plant forms varies as you move from sun to shade and from dry to wet areas. Many native species, and some introduced ones, too, may be found here.

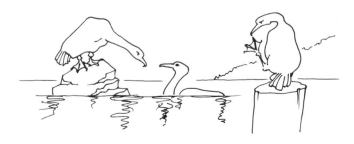

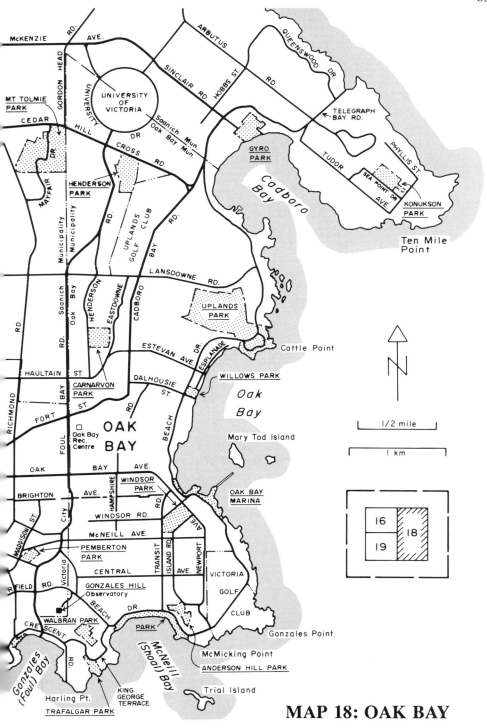

MAP 18: OAK BAY

⟨8⟩ OAK BAY AREA (MAP 18)

Even in established residential areas you can still find places to get off the pavement. Beginning at the northern border of the municipality at the **University of Victoria** lands (see page 61), the "Chip Trip" jogging path around the campus connects with the winding, woodsy trails of the **Henderson Recreation Centre**. Please take care in crossing Cedar Hill Cross Road! The University is also a good setting-off point for hikes up **Mount Tolmie** in Saanich (see page 62).

UPLANDS PARK AND SOUTH:

The Victorienteers (see page 125) have produced a map of the trails (scale 1:3000); price $1.00 to non-members for a photo-copy. The winding trails of the park itself, **Cattle Point** and the walk south to the **Oak Bay Marina** via **Willows Park** provide great urban opportunities for bird-watching and for observing native flora. Spectacular views are possible from the Esplanade: Mount Baker, the Olympic Peninsula, and even Mount Rainier on a clear day.

By following the **Bowker Creek Walkway** from the back of the Oak Bay Recreation Centre east toward the water, and crossing "**Fireman's Park**", you could join this walk along the waterfront.

BRIGHTON AVENUE:

Start off in Victoria's Fairfield neighbourhood at **Pemberton Park**, corner of Gonzales Avenue and Maddison Street. Head north on Maddison to Brighton and turn right. Follow Brighton, as it dead-ends and starts up again, until you reach Hampshire Road. If you are ready for a tea break, **Oak Bay Village** is just two blocks north. Continuing along Brighton, you have just four blocks before a path descends to Transit Road and, via St. Denis Street, **Windsor Park**. Ready for a game of cricket?

Stuart Stark's "Oak Bay's Heritage Buildings", now out of print, would make a wonderful guide to the architecture you'll pass by.

ANDERSON HILL PARK (BLUEBERRY HILL):

Oak Bay's newest park (at only fourteen years) was created from, and is surrounded by, residential property. Even so, it remains a patch of wilderness, carpeted in spring with wild flowers, and a home for nesting birds. (So obey the local bylaw and keep your pet on leash from April 1 to June 30). From the rocky hilltop the views over McNeill (Shoal) Bay and Juan de Fuca Strait are fabulous.

Access is off Island Road from Newport Avenue or from Central Avenue. You may descend along a steep trail to Transit Road, emerging between houses #545 and #577. This is just half a block from the park at McNeill (Shoal) Bay.

GONZALES HILL REGIONAL PARK:
Acquired in 1992, this is the baby in the CRD Parks system. Let's take a look at the old Gonzales Observatory, a weather station for 75 years and now a heritage building. To do so, start out at Gonzales (Foul) Bay's sandy beach and climb the stairs at the eastern end of the beach up to Crescent Road. Keep straight ahead on to King George Terrace then turn left onto Barkley Terrace and climb the stairs to the Observatory, where UVic scientists are gathering data on gases in the atmosphere. After exploring, descend to Fairfield Road along Denison Road; this brings you close to the Victoria/Oak Bay border, where Fairfield Road becomes Beach Drive. From here you can head back to Gonzales Bay via Foul Bay Road, or go on to McNeill Bay via Beach Drive.

WALBRAN PARK:
From the Gonzales Observatory, as described above, you can head east from the parking lot along Denison Road to discover Walbran Park. Climb the stairs to the top to see the cairn dedicated to Juan de Fuca. What a view!

Across the road, look for remnants of a Second World War observation post. From here, look about to discover an unmarked trail descending to a long staircase (signposted at the bottom) that drops to King George Terrace at Sunny Lane. Once again, you are above McNeill Bay, and there is public beach access, via steps, at the end of Sunny Lane.

This completes our sampling of parks and walks in the Oak Bay area. Use of the many back lanes in the older parts of Oak Bay can pleasantly extend many of these walks. For more information please contact:

Oak Bay Municipal Hall, 2167 Oak Bay Ave.
Victoria, BC V8R 1G2
phone 598-3311; fax 598-9108

9 VICTORIA AREA (MAP 19)

There are 158 ha of public parkland in the City of Victoria, divided among 104 parks, large and small, but we have limited ourselves to those areas large enough for you to stretch your legs. At present, 1993, **Thetis Lake Park** (see pages 77-80) is also a Victoria park, although this may change in the near future. For a Victoria parks brochure or for further information please contact:

City of Victoria Parks and Recreation Department at 100 Cook Street (phone 361-0600) or at 633 Pandora Avenue (385-5711)

Mail to: 1 Centennial Square, Victoria, BC V8W 1P6

SUMMIT PARK:

This 4.6-ha park must have the biggest urban blackberry patch in the Victoria area, demonstrating how an introduced plant (in this case the Himalayan blackberry) can overrun an area, destroying native species. Apart from the blackberries and the Scotch broom (another introduced plant), the park is a good example of the rare Garry oak woodland/grass bald habitat. Occuring only on southern Vancouver Island, the Gulf Islands, and in a few isolated patches in the Fraser Valley, it may be the most endangered ecosystem in Canada. One threat is from human encroachment, with trees being cut down. A less obvious form of habitat destruction occurs when property owners water, mow and fertilize natural areas. Between human and plant intrusion, many plants that once thrived in the Garry oak woodland are now endangered or extinct. **The Garry Oak Meadow Preservation Society** has been formed in an effort to protect these precious areas. For up-dated information on the Society contact the Swan Lake/Christmas Hill Nature Sanctuary (see page 54). Man-made features of Summit Park include the Greater Victoria Water District reservoir and a microwave tower. Access is from the end of Highview Street, McNair Street, Summit Avenue, Blackwood Street or The Rise.

PEMBERTON PARK:

This 2-ha neighbourhood park is the setting-off point for the Brighton Avenue walk described on page 64.

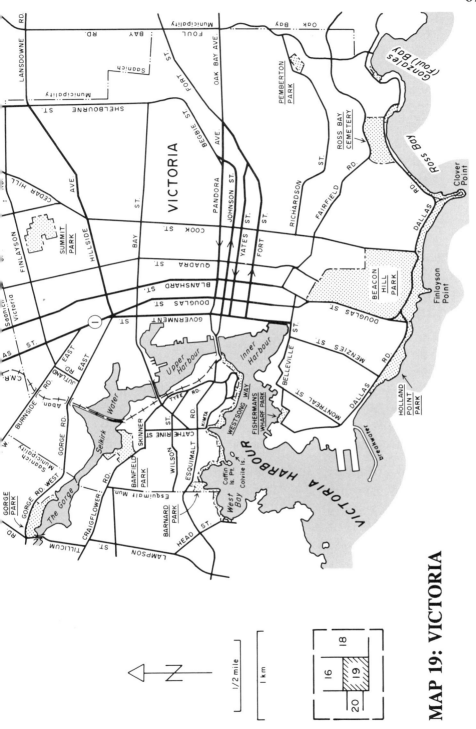

MAP 19: VICTORIA

ROSS BAY CEMETERY:

This 11-ha tombstone cemetery, landscaped with many exotic trees, is the final resting place of many of Victoria's prominent citizens. It is a fine example of a typical Victorian cemetery, with its formal landscaping and artful sculptures. The **Old Cemeteries Society** conducts tours on Sunday afternoons at 2 pm; Tuesday and Thursday at 7 pm, July and August. Meet at Bagga Pasta, 1516 Fairfield Road (Fairfield Plaza). No reservations needed; suggested donation: $5 adults, $3 seniors/students. For information please contact P O Box 40115, Victoria, BC; phone 384-0045. A booklet, "Historic Guide to Ross Bay Cemetery", by John Adams, is available.

BEACON HILL PARK:

Victoria's largest park at close to 75 ha, Beacon Hill Park truly has something for everyone: softball, tennis, lawn bowling, soccer and cricket facilities, a putting green, a petting zoo, playgrounds, a bandshell and so much more, all in a setting of lawns, fields, flower gardens and native and exotic trees.

The Salish name for Beacon Hill was Meeacan, meaning "warmed in the sun" because it looked like a fat man lying on his back to warm his belly in the sunshine. In May each year the hill's south slopes are carpeted in blue camas to create an unforgettable vision. For the Coast Salish, this camas had a more prosaic value as the bulbs were a staple food. For a description of harvesting practices, look to Dr. Nancy J. Turner's "Food Plants of British Columbia".

A booklet entitled "Beacon Hill Park 1882-1982: A Brief History" is available from the City Parks Department for $1.50. The Victorienteers (see page 125) have a 5-colour map of the park (scale 1:5000); price: $5.00 for non-members. To contact the **Friends of Beacon Hill Park,** please phone 389-0938.

HOLLAND POINT TO CLOVER POINT:

This is a world-class stroll! Start off at the Ogden Point breakwater, a popular spot for fishing, scuba-diving, bird-watching and just generally getting wind-blown. Head east, toward Beacon Hill Park, through 5-ha Holland Point Park. The cliffside walk parallels Dallas Road and offers magnificent views of the Olympic Mountains and the Strait of Juan de Fuca. Look for the 'Mile 0' monument at the foot of Douglas Street marking the western terminus of the Trans-Canada Highway, and for plaques marking Victoria Point (site of a gun battery during the Russo-Turkish war), Fonyo Beach (where Steve Fonyo dipped his artificial leg into the Pacific after his cross-Canada run) and the swim of Marilyn Bell (who swam the Strait of Juan de Fuca in 1956). At mid-point in your walk you could stop to rest in the Kiwanis shelter at Finlayson Point or you could detour two blocks up Douglas Street for a soft ice cream cone at the Beacon Drive In Restaurant. As you continue your walk east, watch on your left for what was once the world's tallest totem pole. As you approach Clover Point you are likely to see colourful kites overhead. Take special note of the birds in the air and on the waves: Clover Point is one of the best places around Victoria to spot migrating species.

You could continue your walk on to Ross Bay Cemetery, described above, along a sea-side promenade, spectacular (and sometimes closed) during rough weather. The beach access for Gonzales (Foul) Bay is just a little farther along via Hollywood Crescent and Crescent Road.

INNER HARBOUR:

Start off at **Fishermans Wharf Park** on Erie Street. Enjoy fish and chips from Barb's and a stroll among the moored vessels. Thus fortified, head east toward downtown Victoria. You will immediately need to make a detour, via St. Lawrence Street and Kingston Street, around an undeveloped site (1993). Then look for the public access beside the Coast Victoria Harbourside Hotel at 146 Kingston Street. It continues past the two Harbourside condominium developments and leads to **Laurel Point Park** in front of the Laurel Point Inn. Here you have a 240-degree view of the busy harbour. You will exit through **Centennial Park** (don't miss the totem pole) onto the corner of Belleville Street and Pendray Street. You will need to detour around the terminal for the Black Ball ferry service to Port Angeles, USA, and around the Wax Museum. You are then free to descend to the Lower Causeway and follow the promenade right around to tiny **Reeson Regional Park**, with its "Whaling Wall" mural, and the Johnson Street Bridge (the Blue Bridge). Note the tiny E & N railway station at the east end of the bridge. From here you can explore Old Town or Chinatown, or continue your walk by crossing the Blue Bridge to pick up **Westsong Way**.

WESTSONG WAY:

The combined efforts of the City of Victoria, the Municipality of Esquimalt, BC Enterprise Corporation, the Provincial Capital Commission and property developers have resulted in this spectacular 3.5 km waterfront walkway from the Johnson Street Bridge in Victoria to West Bay in Esquimalt. A plaque at the Victoria end identifies this section as Songhees Way; a section in the middle, by the Royal Quays condominiums, is identified as Mariners Way; and the Esquimalt section has always been known as the West Bay Walkway. In October, 1990, Lieutenant-Governor Lam officially opened the walkway with a combined name of Westsong Way.

Starting from the Johnson Street Bridge and heading west make your way to Songhees Point, then past the Edith Cavell, Kings Landing and Royal Quays condominium developments. Skirt Lime Bay at the foot of Catherine Street (where you will also find Spinnaker's Pub). Next comes Coffin Island Point at the foot of Robert Street. The island just off-shore is Colville Island. As you make your way westward, you leave Victoria at **Barnard Park** and enter Esquimalt. The last section, the **West Bay Walkway**, brings you out to a small parking lot off Head Street, very near to **West Bay Park** (see page 72).

VICTORIA HARBOUR FERRY:

From April to October you can make your exploration of the Inner Harbour and Westsong Way a loop by taking a ride on one of the little ferries that make stops at the Songhees dock; on the Causeway in front of the Empress; in front of Coast Harbourside; at Fishermans Wharf Park in front of Barb's Fish and Chips; and at the West Bay Marina at the foot of Head Street. Information is available at the kiosk on the Causeway, at the Tourist Information Bureau, and at West Bay Marina and R.V. Park, 453 Head St. (phone 385-1831). Ferry service is also available to Ocean Pointe; the foot of Fisgard Street in Chinatown; historical Point Ellice House; **Banfield Park** in Vic West; and **Gorge Park** in Saanich (see page 60).

GALLOPING GOOSE EXTENSION:

See page 76 for a description of the Galloping Goose extension as proposed in 1993. The section that swings south from the Town and Country Shopping Centre in Saanich is about 2.5 km long and takes you through a light-industrial area of Victoria to, and eventually across, the trestle over the Selkirk Water. How the trestle will be modified to allow uninterrupted traffic across it without impeding boat access to The Gorge is currently being discussed. We show the route on our map as Abandoned C.N.R. R/W.

BAYSIDE PROPOSAL:

On the west side of the Selkirk Water between the trestle and the Point Ellice (Bay Street) Bridge lies the former CN Railway Yard, a 4.5-ha parcel owned by CN Real Estate. A current proposal is for redevelopment as Bayside Village, with about one-quarter of the property set aside as public open space, including a walkway.

SELKIRK WATERFRONT PROPOSAL:

On the opposite side of the Selkirk Water, Jawl Holdings has cleared the 9.7-ha former sawmill site (on Gorge Road at the foot of Jutland) for a redevelopment proposal that includes industrial, commercial and residential uses. The current plan includes 1.3 ha of parkland divided between a park in the residential section and a waterfront pathway along the entire shoreline of the project.

DOCKSIDE LANDS:

The City of Victoria owns 11.3 ha, bounded roughly by Esquimalt and Tyee Roads and the Upper Harbour, and stretching from the Johnson Street Bridge to the Point Ellice Bridge. Part of this area is being sold off in several parcels, probably for redevelopment as a business park. Part will remain in public ownership and could include a public corridor to connect the Inner Harbour walkway with the Bayside walkway.

⟨10⟩ ESQUIMALT AREA (MAP 20)

In 1842, James Douglas wrote "Is-shoy-malth" as his interpretation of the native pronunciation. The word may have referred to a local group, the Whyomilth family, or to the "shoaling waters" of the mud flats where the Mill Stream empties into upper Esquimalt Harbour. Dr. Thom Hess of the University of Victoria interviewed local elders, who informed him that the name refers to the narrowing at the head of the harbour, where the water is "squeezed" between its banks.

SAXE POINT PARK:

The entrance to the 6-ha park is at the foot of Fraser Street. This park offers great variety: extensive herbaceous borders, woodland trails, picnic areas and spectacular views. Limited wheelchair access.

FLEMING BEACH, BUXTON GREEN, and
MACAULAY POINT:

Fleming Beach (.8 ha), at the foot of Lampson Street, is home to the Esquimalt Angler's Association and is the gateway to Buxton Green, a perfect picnic area. Adjacent Macaulay Point (4.86 ha) is leased from the Department of National Defence and developed as parkland with great views of Victoria, the Olympic Mountains and Juan de Fuca Strait. Limited wheelchair access.

HIGHROCK CAIRN PARK:

Much of the 4.75-ha park has been left in a natural state. Climb the hill to the cairn lookout: the views are fantastic. Wheelchair access difficult.

KINSMEN GORGE PARK:

On Tillicum Road, just over the Gorge Bridge from Saanich, lies this 13-ha multi-use park. There's something for everyone: swimming, picnicking, tennis, and paths alongside the Gorge waterway. Wheelchair accessible.

WEST BAY PARK and WEST BAY WALKWAY:

West Bay Park, next to the nautical blue and white house at 507 Head Street, is a perfect spot for a picnic before heading off on the Walkway, which starts from a small parking lot on Head Street between Dunsmuir and Gore. This was the first section to be completed of what later was re-named **Westsong Way** (see page 70). Some sections are not wheelchair accessible. If you should spot a Purple Martin you can thank the local nest-box program. Call Darren Copley at 479-9879 for details.

For more information on these and other parks in the area, please contact:

Esquimalt Parks and Recreation Commission
527 Fraser Street, Victoria, BC V9A 6H6
phone 386-6128

MAP 20: ESQUIMALT

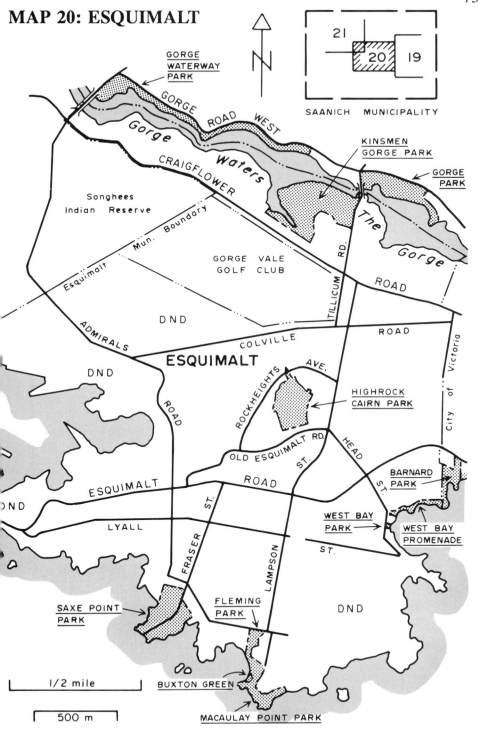

SAANICH MUNICIPALITY

GORGE WATERWAY PARK

KINSMEN GORGE PARK

GORGE PARK

GORGE ROAD WEST

Gorge Waters

CRAIGFLOWER

Songhees Indian Reserve

Esquimalt Mun. Boundary

The Gorge

GORGE VALE GOLF CLUB

TILLICUM RD.

ROAD

DND

ADMIRALS

ROAD

COLVILLE ROAD

ESQUIMALT

DND

City of Victoria

ROAD

ROCKHEIGHTS AVE.

HIGHROCK CAIRN PARK

OLD ESQUIMALT RD.

ST.

HEAD ST.

BARNARD PARK

ESQUIMALT ROAD

ST.

WEST BAY PARK

WEST BAY PROMENADE

DND

LYALL

FRASER ST.

LAMPSON ST.

ST.

SAXE POINT PARK

FLEMING PARK

DND

1/2 mile

BUXTON GREEN

500 m

MACAULAY POINT PARK

⟨11⟩ VIEW ROYAL AREA (MAP 21)

View Royal was named after a 1912 subdivision of land originally purchased by Dr. John S. Helmcken in 1851. Promoters of the subdivision claimed the lots had a "royal view." From the time of early settlement the development of this area has been influenced by the roads running through it. The Four Mile House and the Six Mile House Hotel were originally stopping places on the road from Fort Victoria to farms located as far west as Sooke. Later, they were to serve the miners travelling to and from the gold workings at Leechtown.

PORTAGE MUNICIPAL PARK:

Portage Park, with its woodland trails, beach, and archaeological sites, is just off the Old Island Highway near the "Four Mile Hill." Here you'll find the Four Mile House, now a tearoom, restaurant and pub. Peter and Elizabeth (Montgomery) Calvert had it built as a farm house but before long it became a small inn.

Steep stairs make wheelchair access to the park impossible. Entrance to the park is gained through the town hall parking lot:

Town of View Royal
45 View Royal Avenue
Victoria, BC V9B 1A6
phone 479-6800; fax 727-9551

VIEW ROYAL MUNICIPAL PARK:

The entrance to View Royal Park is at the corner of Helmcken Road and Pheasant Lane, just where the E & N railway crosses Helmcken. Craigflower Creek skirts one side of the park, offering pleasant picnic spots. A level chip trail around the perimeter of the park is especially suitable for jogging and there is a playground for children. Wheelchair accessible.

WATERS EDGE WALKWAY:

From the north end of Parson's Bridge it is possible to locate rough stairs leading down to a walkway between the Waters Edge residential development and the upper reaches of Esquimalt Harbour. At present it is just a short walk, and you must return the way you came, but it marks the start of what View Royal hopes will become a series of public accesses along its shoreline. The next addition should come just on the other side of Parson's Bridge when the Six Mile House

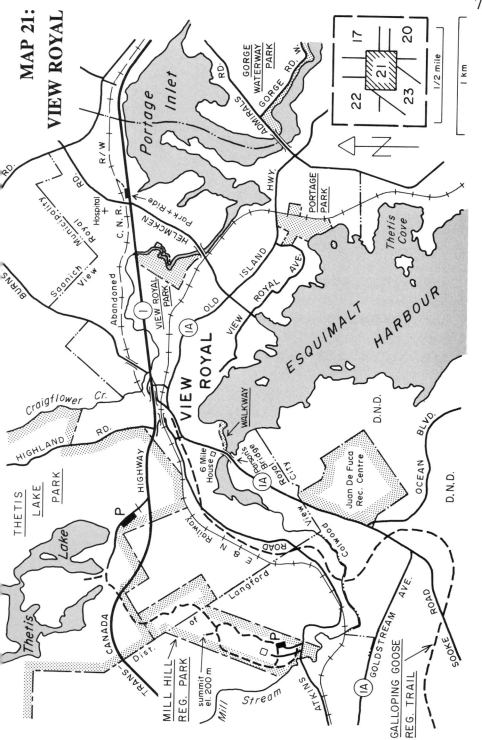

75

MAP 21:
VIEW ROYAL

land is re-developed. The bridge is named for William Richard Parson who first purchased a liquor licence for his Parsons Bridge Hotel in 1856. The inn was well situated, being close to the first sawmill and to the Mill Stream, where ships' water barrels were refilled. The Esquimalt naval station was established nearby in 1864, providing thirsty patrons to join the travellers on their way to and from Colwood, Langford, Metchosin and Sooke.

GALLOPING GOOSE EXTENSION

From the Atkins Road parking lot which marks the eastern end of the Galloping Goose Regional Trail (see below), the CNR right-of-way continues on, through Saanich and into Victoria. In 1993 it was proposed that this 9.5 km section become an extension of the Galloping Goose Trail. We show it on our map as Abandoned C.N.R. R/W. Through View Royal and into Saanich the right-of-way roughly parallels the Trans-Canada Highway to the Town and Country Shopping Centre. At this point it splits into two spurs. The one heading north past Swan Lake to McKenzie Avenue (2 km) is known as the Saanich Spur (see page 56 and Map 16). The one heading south leads to the Vic West area of Victoria via a trestle over the Selkirk Water (see pages 70-71 and Map 19).

GALLOPING GOOSE REGIONAL TRAIL

This 47-km section of Canadian National Railway (CNR) right-of-way, from Atkins Road to the Alberni Canal, was originally part of the Canadian Northern Pacific Railway which had been built across the Prairies. The section from Victoria to Leechtown was started in 1911. The CNR took over the entire Canadian Northern Railway in 1920. The line was used mostly for transporting logs and freight but passenger service ran from Victoria to Sooke starting in 1922, was extended to Youbou in 1925 and ceased in 1931. Passenger service was by a gasoline-powered railbus known as the "Galloping Goose". This type of coach was used throughout Canada and commemorated on a postage stamp in the 1980s. One person handled all the duties of engineer, conductor and baggage handler. Although use of the line declined around the 1930s, the Victoria-Deerholme section was used up until the 1970s: munitions were transported to Rocky Point, and poles were carried from Leechtown to a poleyard at Milne's Landing. This service ended in 1979 and by 1982 the rails had been removed.

In 1987 an agreement was reached between the Province of BC and the CRD to lease this section of the abandoned CNR right-of-way for regional park use for twenty-one years (until 2008). Over the last 20 years, many groups have had a part in preserving the corridor; it now forms part of the Regional Trail System (see page 123), and is recognized in the Official Community Plans of View Royal, Colwood, Langford, Metchosin and Sooke. The Galloping Goose Trail offers pleasant urban walks and, although never far from a highway, it removes one from the hurly-burly, with surprising glimpses of animal life, hedgerow flowers in season and some beautiful lookout points. Many trails lead off from the right-of-way but please resist the temptation to stray onto private lands. Once out to Metchosin the trail leads you to or through several public parks.

No motorized vehicles are permitted, but hikers, horse riders and cyclists share the trail. Courtesy between user groups is encouraged, with cycling clubs giving the right-of-way to hikers, and with hikers giving way to equestrians. Dogs should be kept on a lead and under control at all times.

Many sections, particularly the section near the Luxton Fairgrounds, are suitable for wheelchair use but the only wheelchair accessible toilets are at Roche Cove Regional Park.

Note that the two high trestles on the section from Charters Creek to Leechtown are posted as closed to public use until repairs can be completed. Formerly, the Sooke River Railway Preservation Society operated a railway service along part of this section; many were saddened to see this service end. Contact CRD Parks (see page 126) for updated information on this and other sections of the Galloping Goose Regional Trail.

THETIS LAKE PARK (MAP 22)

Travelling about 9 km west on Highway 1 brings you to Thetis Lake Park (661 ha). From late May to late August, paid parking at the main lot generates funds for the maintenance of the park. Elsewhere, there is limited parking only. The park is spectacular for its many wild flowers in spring, outcrops of moss-covered bedrock, arbutus, Garry oak and Douglas-fir. Park facilities include a swimming area, change room and toilets. Power boats and camping are prohibited. Cycling is permitted only on fire roads at least 3 m wide.

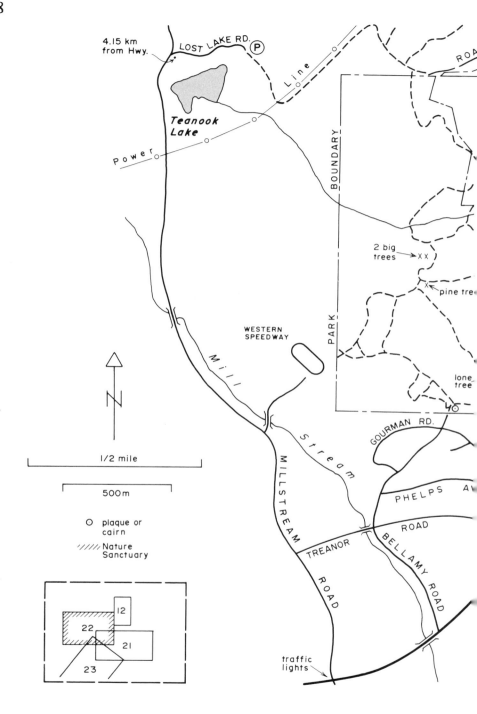

MAP 22: THETIS LAKE PARK

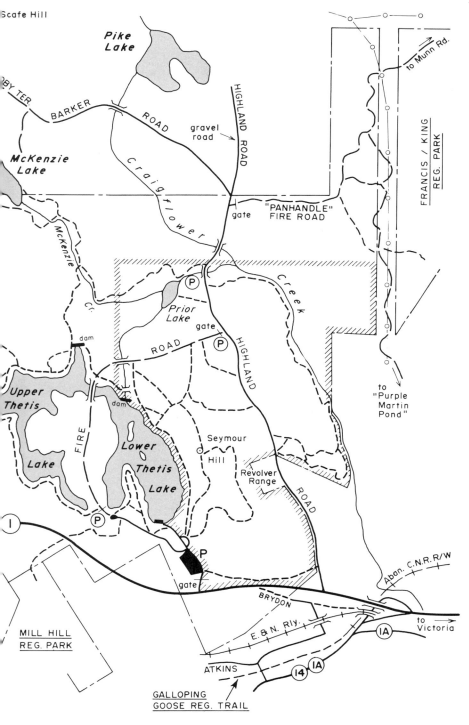

Scafe Hill

Pike Lake

BARKER ROAD

BY TER.

McKenzie Lake

Craigflower

HIGHLAND ROAD

gravel road

gate

"PANHANDLE" FIRE ROAD

Creek

FRANCIS / KING REG. PARK

to Munn Rd.

McKenzie Cr.

dam

P

Prior Lake

ROAD

gate

P

HIGHLAND

Upper Thetis

FIRE

dam

Lower Thetis Lake

Seymour Hill

Revolver Range

ROAD

to "Purple Martin Pond"

Lake

I

P

P

gate

BRYDON

Aban. C.N.R. R/W

MILL HILL REG. PARK

E. & N. Rly.

ATKINS

14

IA

IA

to Victoria

GALLOPING GOOSE REG. TRAIL

For a short one-hour hike, follow the trail just east of Lower Lake to the bridge at the junction of the lakes then the fire road back to the parking area. Allow two hours to hike around both lakes. The high trail east of Lower Lake leads up onto Seymour Hill to a cairn and good viewpoint.

The area west of the lakes has numerous unmarked trails. Access is possible via Bellamy Road; off Phelps Avenue; via Millstream Road at Lost Lake Road; and via Highland Road at Barker Road (where parking space is very limited indeed). Going northwest from the Upper Lake an excellent hike can be made to Scafe Hill, with good views from both its summits. From here, with pre-arranged transportation, one can hike out to Millstream Road.

The City of Victoria currently (1993) administers the park, with trail maintenance help from members of the **Thetis Park Nature Sanctuary Association** (also known as the Friends of Thetis Lake Park). Their booklet "Natural History of Thetis Lake Park near Victoria, British Columbia" is available from the Field-Naturalist store, 1241 Broad Street, Victoria. Membership information is available by calling 598-3417.

Ron Seaborn is credited with earlier mapping of the trails in the park. A map of the trails, along with a guide to wild flowers, is located at the Jessie Woollett Memorial, near the main entrance to the park, and the Victorienteers (see page 125) have produced a coloured contour map of the park. Price: $5.00 to non-members.

Note:

- Trails lead to Freeman King Park, to Mill Hill Park, and to the Galloping Goose Regional Trail. Hikers are cautioned, however, to avoid trying to cross Highway 1.

- Be careful with fire. The moss gets very dry in summer and is easily ignited.

- Please take out your garbage. • **Don't pick the flowers.**

⟨12⟩ LANGFORD and COLWOOD AREAS (MAP 23)

In this book, the newly-incorporated (December, 1992) District of Langford is combined with the City of Colwood because the Galloping Goose Trail snakes back and forth between the two. For information on local parks please contact:

District of Langford
2805 Carlow Road
Victoria, BC V9B 5V9
phone 478-7882

City of Colwood
3300 Wishart Road
Victoria, BC V9C 1R1
phone 478-5590

GOLDSTREAM PROVINCIAL PARK (MAP 32)

The park is fully within the District of Langford, but it is your gateway to the scenically spectacular Malahat Drive, so we have placed it in section ⟨19⟩ Malahat Area. Please turn to page 117.

MILL HILL REGIONAL PARK (MAPS 21 and 23)

From Victoria on Highway 1 (Trans-Canada Highway) travel 9 km to the Thetis highway interchange. Take the Colwood underpass and the first right turn at the sign for Atkins Road (where you will find the parking lot for the start of the Galloping Goose Regional Trail). Continue along Atkins 3 km and watch for the Mill Hill park sign on the right. Or, you can travel Highway 1 for 12 km to the traffic lights at Millstream Road and turn left. Just before the shopping district turn left again at the Atkins Avenue sign. Continue over Mill Stream Bridge; then, immediately after the turnoff to CRD Parks Headquarters, turn left to the large parking lot.

Evidence of shell middens can be found near the base of the Summit Trail. Before European contact, the Songhees people camped at the mouth of the Mill Stream. Later, the Mill Stream waters supplied the power for the first sawmill on Vancouver Island, which was located at Esquimalt Harbour near Parson's Bridge. It was in operation as early as 1848.

Mill Hill Park (49 ha) is a good place for early spring flowers, and in the shaded areas you will find the calypso orchid. For a field checklist of the wild flowers found in the park, contact CRD Parks (see page 126). Time up to the viewpoint on the Calypso Trail is about 20 minutes. From the 200-m summit, the site of an old lookout tower, there are magnificent views in all directions.

82

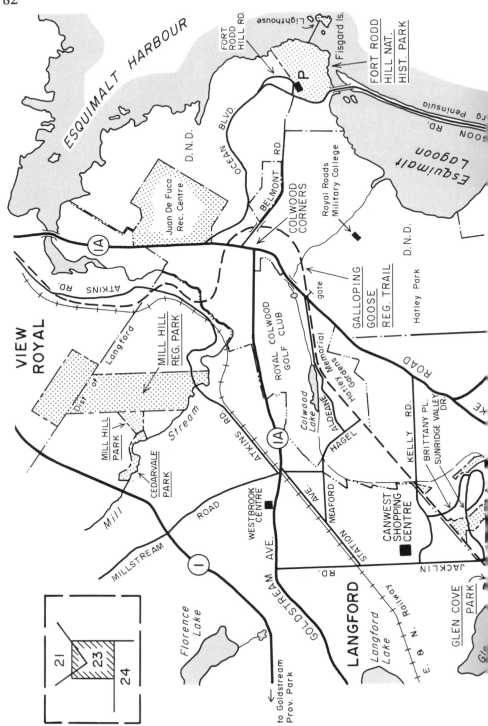

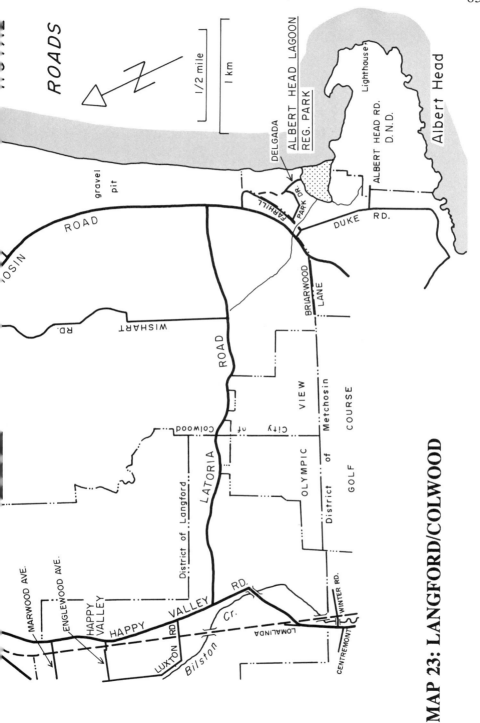

ROADS

1/2 mile

1 km

ALBERT HEAD LAGOON
REG. PARK

DELGADA

Lighthouse

ALBERT HEAD RD.
D.N.D.

Albert Head

gravel pit

ROAD

OSIN

FARHILL

PARK DR.

DUKE RD.

WISHART RD.

RD.

BRIARWOOD LANE

ROAD

LATORIA

Colwood

District of Langford

City of Colwood

VIEW

OLYMPIC

District of Metchosin

GOLF COURSE

MARWOOD AVE.

ENGLEWOOD AVE.

HAPPY VALLEY

HAPPY VALLEY RD.

LUXTON RD

Bilston Cr.

LOMALINDA

WINTER RD.

CENTREMONT

MAP 23: LANGFORD/COLWOOD

Picnic tables and toilets are near the parking lot. Trails are not wheelchair accessible.

There are no bridle or bike trails. In this Nature Appreciation Park, all dogs must be on leash.

GALLOPING GOOSE REGIONAL TRAIL: Thetis highway interchange to Colwood Corners (MAP 23)

For access, see **Mill Hill Regional Park** above; for a description of the Galloping Goose Trail, see page 76. The highlight of this 3-km section is the Mill Stream, crossed by a sturdy bridge near the falls, which are especially lovely on cold, bright days in winter.

JUAN DE FUCA RECREATION CENTRE (MAP 23)

1767 Island Highway, Victoria, BC V9B 1J1; phone 478-8384

In addition to the pool and ice arena buildings visible from the highway, the Centre has golf, baseball, tennis, soccer and more. It is also home to the velodrome and lawn bowling facilities for the 1994 Commonwealth Games. For joggers and hikers there is a chip trail around the perimeter of the 40-ha grounds and a loop path around the high ground near the highway. A favorite but unofficial use of the grounds is for tobogganing when Victoria gets a snowfall.

The Victorienteers (see page 125) have produced a colour contour map (scale 1:6000), price $5.00 to non-members.

FORT RODD HILL and FISGARD LIGHTHOUSE NATIONAL HISTORIC SITES (MAP 23)

603 Fort Rodd Hill Road, Victoria, BC V9C 2W8

Open daily 10:00 am–5:30 pm (limited services Oct. 15–Apr. 1). Free admission. Phone 363-4662 for a recorded message before planning a visit. Access is via Highway 1A and Ocean Boulevard.

For several years, band concerts have been given each Sunday at 2 pm by the band of the 5th (British Columbia) Field Regiment, Royal Canadian Artillery. As Victoria's oldest military unit, "The Fifth" provided militia artillerymen from 1878 to 1956 to man the guns of the Victoria and Esquimalt defences, including those at Fort Rodd Hill.

Fort Rodd Hill and the Fisgard Lighthouse are great places to explore and have a picnic. Be prepared, though, to share the grassy slopes with the resident deer.

ESQUIMALT LAGOON (MAP 23)

Just a short distance farther along Ocean Boulevard brings you to the Esquimalt Lagoon. As you walk the length of the Coburg Peninsula, on one side you have the open ocean and on the other the sheltered waters of the Esquimalt Lagoon, a Waterfowl Sanctuary; both offer great opportunities for bird-watching, especially at times of migration. Inland, across the lagoon, one can see the buildings and grounds of Hatley Park (see below).

GALLOPING GOOSE REGIONAL TRAIL:
Colwood Corners to Hatley Park (MAP 23)

There is no pedestrian crosswalk at Sooke Road and Aldeane, so this section is probably best enjoyed as an extension of a visit to Hatley Park, described next.

HATLEY PARK–ROYAL ROADS MILITARY COLLEGE (MAP 23)

Hatley Castle, in the 263-ha Hatley Park estate, was designed by Victoria architect Samuel McClure and completed in 1908 for James Dunsmuir, premier of BC from 1900 to 1902 and lieutenant-governor of the province from 1906 to 1909. James was the son of Robert Dunsmuir, the Scottish coal baron who built Craigdarroch Castle, and was himself a very wealthy man. Hatley Castle cost four million dollars to build. The gardens, planted in 1910, were designed by Brett & Hall landscape architects of Boston, and required 100 workers. James died in 1920, and his wife Laura, in 1937. In 1940 the castle and the surrounding square mile of grounds were purchased by the federal government for seventy-five thousand dollars. The estate is now occupied by Royal Roads Military College, a degree-granting university for Canadian officers. The castle and buildings are closed to the public, but the grounds are open 10 am to 4 pm daily, subject to restrictions when dignitaries are visiting—you may want to call ahead to the gate. The grounds are attractive and varied, with ponds and streams, Italian and Japanese gardens, and resident peacocks.

For information please contact:

> **Royal Roads Military College** Sooke Road, Victoria (mail:
> FMO, Victoria, BC, V0S 1B0); phone 363-4660 (office),
> 363-4634 (gate).

The Victorienteers (see page 125) have produced a colour map (scale 1:10,000); price $5.00 to non-members.

While you are at Hatley Park, include a visit to **Colwood Creek**. Park in the main visitors parking lot and head down the main road. Just before a road branches off to the left, look for an unmarked trail on your left. It descends into the shady valley where you can follow the creek for some distance until your way is blocked and you must turn to retrace your steps. This idyllic spot is worth a visit.

For a second view of the creek, continue down the road to the sign for the Glen Gardens and trail. A steep descent through the recently developed gardens brings you down to creek level, where you can follow a woodsy trail out to Esquimalt Lagoon. You can circle back to the parking lot by way of the Castle gardens.

GALLOPING GOOSE REGIONAL TRAIL:
Hatley Park to Happy Valley (MAP 23)

Two parks in the vicinity of Glen Lake afford opportunities to step off the Galloping Goose to explore or take a lunch break. The first is **Colwood Creek Park**. Turn onto Brittany Drive where it crosses the trail near the Canwest Shopping Centre and follow Brittany around to its intersection with Sunridge Valley Drive. Enter the park and take the bridge across Colwood Creek to the main, open area of the park. You'll find picnic tables and playground equipment for the children. After crossing the creek again, pick up the trail on the other side of Sunridge Valley Drive. You'll regain the Galloping Goose Trail just behind Belmont School. Another small park is **Glen Cove Park** at the foot of Glen Lake, a second opportunity to step off the Galloping Goose for a break.

When Langford incorporated in 1992, the 428-ha **Happy Valley** area (see Contents Map) was not included, so it remains an unorganized area within the CRD, but outside the boundaries of the three neighbouring municipalities of Langford, Colwood and Metchosin.

⟨13⟩ METCHOSIN AREA (MAP 24)

The original inhabitants of this area called it "Smets-shosin", meaning "place of stinking fish" after a time when a dead whale was washed up on shore. James Douglas recorded it as "Metcho-sin", and it has come to us as Metchosin.

The District of Metchosin has so far managed to retain its rural charm for the pleasure of residents and visitors alike. Some of the prettiest stretches of the Galloping Goose Regional Trail (see page 76) are to be found in Metchosin, and most of our other hikes in this area could be combined with a section of the Galloping Goose to stretch your legs a bit further. For more information please contact:

District of Metchosin
4450 Happy Valley Road, R R 4 Victoria, BC V9B 5T8
phone 474-3167

ALBERT HEAD LAGOON REGIONAL PARK (MAPS 23 and 24)

To reach Albert Head Lagoon from Victoria, take Highways 1A (Old Island Highway) and 14 (Sooke Road). Turn left onto Metchosin Road, travel 4 km and turn left onto Farhill Road just before reaching the far end of the gravel pit. Turn right at the first junction and proceed to the end of the road: Farhill becomes Park Drive becomes Delgada Road. Resist any temptation to try to drive off the road or your vehicle will become bogged down in sand and gravel. In 1993 a gate, to be locked between 10 pm and 7 am, was installed across the lower end of Delgada Road. Parking is limited and there are no facilities at this park. This is a nature sanctuary and a CRD Nature Appreciation Park so all dogs must be on leash.

Just north of the parking lot is the site of the second sawmill on Vancouver Island, a steam powered mill constructed for the Vancouver's Island Steam Sawmill Company in 1853. The sawmill suffered many financial and mechanical difficulties before burning to the ground in 1859. The earlier inhabitants, the Stsangal band, had fared no better: considered a lower class people, they were raided for slaves by other bands.

Only 7 ha in size, the park encircles a picture-perfect lagoon which is almost closed off by its gravel berm. Take along your favourite field

MAP 24:
METCHOSIN

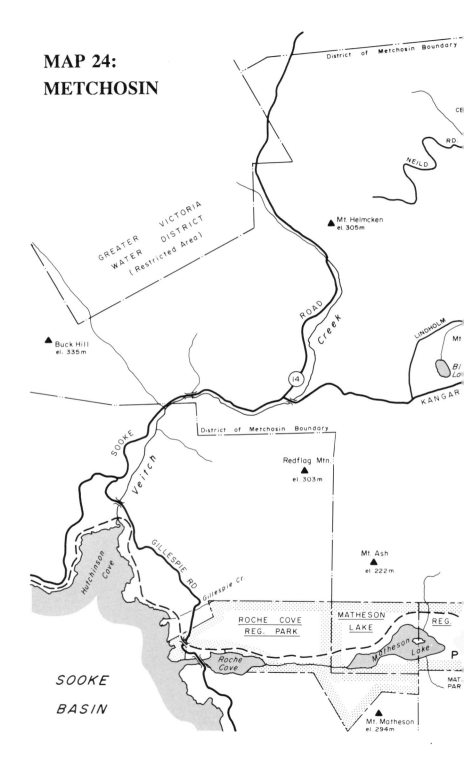

District of Metchosin Boundary

GREATER VICTORIA
WATER DISTRICT
(Restricted Area)

NEILD
CE
RD.

Mt. Helmcken
el. 305m

ROAD
Creek

LINDHOLM
Mt
Bi
La

Buck Hill
el. 335m

14

KANGAR

SOOKE

Veitch

District of Metchosin Boundary

Redflag Mtn.
el. 303m

Mt. Ash
el 222m

GILLESPIE RD.

Hutchinson Cove

Gillespie Cr.

ROCHE COVE
REG. PARK

MATHESON
LAKE

REG.

P

Matheson Lake

MAT.
PAR

Roche
Cove

SOOKE

BASIN

Mt. Matheson
el 294m

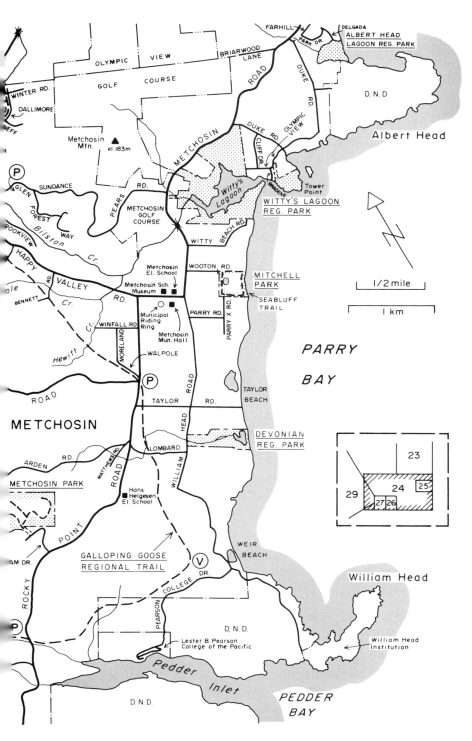

FARHILL

PARK DR.

DELGADA
ALBERT HEAD
LAGOON REG. PARK

BRIARWOOD
LANE

OLYMPIC   VIEW

GOLF   COURSE

WINTER RD.

DALLIMORE

NEFF

METCHOSIN   ROAD

DUKE   RD.

D. N. D.

Albert Head

Metchosin
Mtn.   ▲
el.183m

DUKE RD.

OLYMPIC
VIEW

CLIFF DR.

P

SUNDANCE

GLEN

FOREST   WAY

BROOKVIEW

Billson   Cr.

PEARS   RD.

METCHOSIN
GOLF
COURSE

Witty's
Lagoon

BRADENE

Tower
Point

WITTY'S LAGOON
REG. PARK

HAPPY   RD.

VALLEY

BENNETT

Cr.

WITTY   BEACH RD.

WITTY

WOOTON   RD.

Metchosin
El. School

Metchosin Sch.
Museum ■ ■

MITCHELL
PARK

SEABLUFF
TRAIL

ole

WINFALL RD.

MORELAND

Hewitt

Municipal
Riding
Ring

Metchosin
Mun. Hall

PARRY RD.

PARRY X RD.

P

WALPOLE

ROAD

TAYLOR   RD.

HEAD

ROAD

TAYLOR
BEACH

PARRY

BAY

ROAD

METCHOSIN

ARDEN   RD.

LOMBARD

MATTHEWS RD.

WILLIAM

DEVONIAN
REG. PARK

METCHOSIN PARK

POINT

ROAD

Hans
Helgesen
El. School ■

WEIR
BEACH

AM DR.

GALLOPING GOOSE
REGIONAL TRAIL

V   DR.

ROCKY

PEARSON   COLLEGE   DR.

William Head

P

D. N. D.

Lester B. Pearson
College of the Pacific

William Head
Institution

Pedder   Inlet

D. N. D.

PEDDER
BAY

1/2 mile

1 km

23

29

24   25

27 26

guides; see how many plants you can find along the berm, and how many birds you can identify around the lagoon. (Keep an eye out for mute swans and migrating waterfowl.) A short walk north along the cobble beach is possible.

MITCHELL PARK/SEABLUFF TRAIL (MAP 24)

A new hike in Metchosin is the Seabluff Trail, donated by Geoff and B. H. Mitchell, long-time Metchosin residents. It is a short hike around open fields, along sea view bluffs (50 m high, looking south to the Olympics), and through woods, skirting a small irrigation pond. Please do not disturb the sheep; dogs MUST be on a leash at all times; leave gates closed. Please note that only the perimeter trail is park. The open space in the centre is part of an operating farm. Please do not hike over this area.

Access is by Metchosin and Wooton Roads or by William Head, Parry and Parry Cross Roads.

DEVONIAN REGIONAL PARK (MAP 24)

Access from Victoria is by Highways 1, 1A and 14, then by Metchosin Road and William Head Road, about 50 minutes' drive from Victoria. About 500 m beyond Taylor Road you will find Devonian Park (13 ha) with an ample parking lot (gated) and a picnic area.

In 1857, John McGregor purchased a parcel of land (Section 5, Metchosin District), from the government of the Colony of Vancouver Island, which included the present day park, and here he established his home which he named "Oakwood". The McGregor's two youngest daughters, Agnes and Jean Katherine (Kate), were both born there. The eldest daughter, Mary, who had been born in Scotland in 1845, was married at "Oakwood" on March 12, 1861, to John Van Houten of the Sandwich Islands (Hawaii).

On November 12, 1862, Hans Lars Helgesen married Lillian Colquhoun in Victoria; on January 13, 1863, they purchased "Oakwood" and renamed it "Sherwood". Here seven children were born to the Helgesens. Two of the sons died at an early age and were buried on the farm. Their remains were later exhumed and reburied in the new St. Mary's church cemetery which opened in 1873. Many descendants of the Helgesen family still live in the Metchosin area.

In 1980, through the generosity of the Devonian Foundation and the provincial government, the CRD acquired 11.3 ha comprising Devonian Regional Park. The CRD purchased an additional 2.2 ha in 1983 to provide for the Helgesen bridle trail along the park boundary.

Sherwood Pond used to be one of the many lagoons found along the Metchosin coast. Its barrier spit eventually closed off the lagoon, leaving it, and its population of cutthroat trout, landlocked. Usually trout fry leave for the ocean in their second or third year, and return to spawn in their fourth. This population has adapted to fresh water for life. The cobble barrier is porous enough to allow some passage of water, so the level of the pond can vary by as much as 2 metres. Year round the pond is a delight for birdwatchers.

Allow about 25 minutes to reach the beach from the parking lot. Tides permitting, a 3-km-one-way walk is possible from Taylor Beach (a shelving, pebble beach) to Witty's Lagoon. Note that there is also beach access at Taylor Road.

The steep trails and the toilet facilities are not wheelchair accessible, but the picnic area could be.

This is a CRD Nature Appreciation Park so all dogs must be on a leash.

METCHOSIN WILDERNESS PARK (MAP 24)

Metchosin has been granted a licence of occupancy for Section 25, known also as Clapham Park and Hundred Acre Park. Located northwest of Rocky Point Road between Arden Road and Clapham Drive, its trails are shared by hikers and horseback riders. There are several viewpoints and its deep woods and small creeks offer an excellent shady hike for a hot day.

From the Clapham Drive access follow the main trail, keeping right to the viewpoint. Or, bearing left from the access, cross the sturdy wooden bridge. The trail ahead eventually leads out of the park onto private lands. Turning right after the bridge takes one to the Arden Road access. From the Arden access, take the first left (and cross a bridge) and later a second bridge to a "T", left to the viewpoint or right to Clapham Drive.

BLINKHORN LAKE (MAP 24)

Blinkhorn Lake is a pleasant spot to visit, with a woodsy trail encircling the picturesque lake. (Turn left at the red gate.) Access is off Kangaroo Road. It is Greater Victoria Water District property but is not closed to the public.

WITTY'S LAGOON REGIONAL PARK (MAPS 24 and 25)

Access from Victoria is via Highways 1, 1A and 14, then turn onto Metchosin Road. Follow this for about 6 km to Pears Road and the Metchosin Golf and Country Club (open to the public). Opposite, on the left, is the main entrance to the park, where there is ample parking, toilet facilities and, in 1993, a temporary CRD Nature House. Allow about 45 minutes' driving time from Victoria. Other more limited parking areas are shown on the map, principally at Olympic View Drive and at the end of Witty Beach Road.

This was the site of the village of the Ka-Ky-Aakan band in the 1850s when the first settlers arrived. Metchosin was purchased from this band by the Hudson's Bay Company by agreement (the Douglas Treaties) dated May 1, 1850, by which the band received the equivalent in blankets of £43/6/8. The village was abandoned in the early 1860s when the few surviving members, most of mixed Clallum blood but practiced in Songhees ways and traditions, moved to Esquimalt to join the main Songhees tribe whose jurisdiction extended from William Head to Sayward Beach and the D'Arcy Islands.

The park (56 ha) was originally created in 1969 and became a CRD park in 1986. The old Nature House, never designed as such, was closed in January, 1992. Development of a management plan for the park was begun in 1992. Some of the issues the plan addresses are handling of introduced species, wildlife trees (see note below) and archaeological sites. Witty's is a nature appreciation park: here you will find an interesting combination of forest, grassland, salt marsh, beach, lagoon and rocky shore, with many birds and plants in these various habitats. This is one place where you may find cyclamen growing wild. Sitting Lady Falls can be spectacular in winter and spring after heavy rain.

Tides permitting, a hike along the beach from here to Taylor Road or Devonian Park is possible.

MAP 25: WITTY'S LAGOON REGIONAL PARK

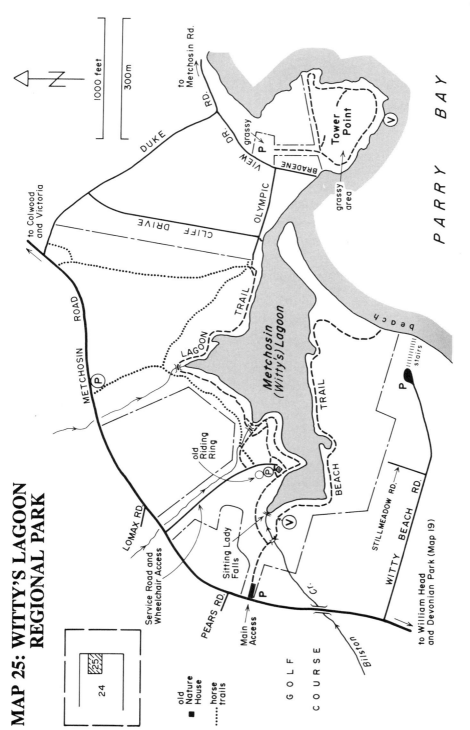

Horses should stay on the designated horse trails or roads; bikes are prohibited throughout the park. Dogs must be kept under control at all times.

For information on access to the wheelchair-accessible picnic area, washrooms and trails, please contact CRD Parks, 478-3344.

Tower Point, accessible from Olympic View Drive off Duke Road, is a part of Witty's Lagoon Park. In winter the grass parking area is gated and locked so you must park on the road. From the Tower Point trails you have a front-row view of harbour seals on the rocks just off shore. The pocket beaches on the west side of the point are excellent places to study pillow basalt, formed about 55 million years ago when molten rock (magma) was cooled by ocean waters. The picnic area, with a water tap and picnic tables, is wheelchair accessible, but the trails and toilets are not.

Note:

Wildlife trees are old, dead or decaying trees used by wildlife for nesting, food, shelter, denning, roosting and perching. For more information about wildlife trees or a pamphlet, "Hanging Wildlife Tree Signs", please contact:

> **Wildlife Tree Coordinator**
> c/o Integrated Management Branch
> Ministry of Environment, Lands and Parks
> 780 Blanshard St., Victoria, BC V8V 1X4

MATHESON LAKE PARK (MAPS 24 and 26)

Access from Victoria is via Highway 14—Metchosin Road—Happy Valley Road—and Rocky Point Road (29 km). Just before the road forks, turn right onto Matheson Lake Park Road (signposted) and about 1.5 km brings you to the parking lot (gated and locked 9 pm–8 am).

For many years a provincial park, Matheson Lake Park (160 ha) was scheduled to be transferred to the Capital Regional District in 1993.

In addition to hiking, there is swimming and some fishing. The southeast corner of the lake is the best place to launch canoes, but motor boats are not allowed.

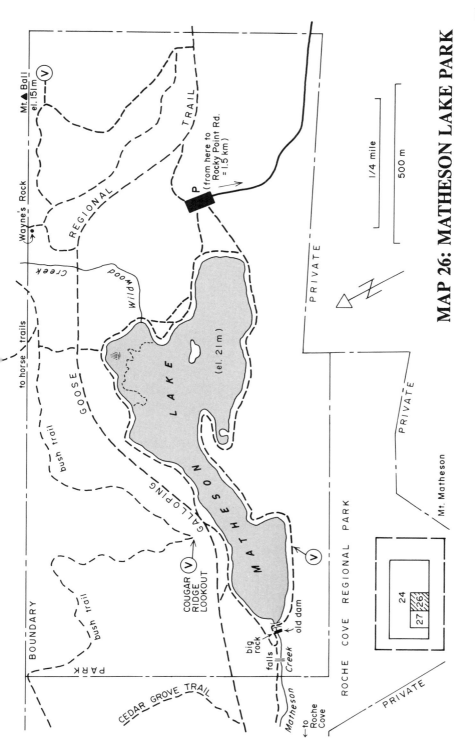

MAP 26: MATHESON LAKE PARK

Mt. Ball el. 151m

Wayne's Rock

REGIONAL TRAIL

(from here to Rocky Point Rd. = 1.5 km)

P

Creek

Wildwood

to horse trails

GOOSE

bush trail

LAKE

(el. 21 m)

GALLOPING

MATHESON

BOUNDARY

PARK

bush trail

COUGAR RIDGE LOOKOUT

CEDAR GROVE TRAIL

big rock

old dam

falls

Matheson Creek

to Roche Cove

ROCHE COVE REGIONAL PARK

Mt. Matheson

PRIVATE

PRIVATE

PRIVATE

N

1/4 mile

500 m

24

27 26

The Galloping Goose Regional Trail links the park to Roche Cove (4.5 km one way). Trails circle Matheson Lake, and from the Galloping Goose at Wildwood Creek a trail leads up to Wayne's Rock (about 15 minutes' walk). Wildwood Creek has three forks and in the area just north of our map several horse trails have been developed. Just beyond Wayne's Rock a trail leads west over the creek and in 15 minutes brings you again to the Galloping Goose Trail.

Trails lead up to Mount Ball from whose summit the view is northward to Mount Redflag. A good viewpoint is also shown on our map towards Victoria and the sea.

The trail along the creek from Matheson Lake to Roche Cove was the old timers' portage trail in the 1850s and '60s.

No camping; no fires; no cycling. Pets must be on a leash.

⟨14⟩ EAST SOOKE AREA (CONTENTS MAP)

East Sooke is an unincorporated area within the Capital Regional District. It contains two of the large CRD parks, Roche Cove and East Sooke Regional parks:

ROCHE COVE REGIONAL PARK (MAPS 24 and 27)

Access to Roche Cove Regional Park (117 ha) is by Highway 14. Just past 17 Mile House turn left onto Gillespie Road and 3 km will bring you to the parking lot with wheelchair-accessible toilet facilities. It is about a 45-minute drive from Victoria.

Cross the road and go on foot past the barrier to the walk-in picnic area. The road ahead leads to the coast past the caretaker's residence on your left. Yellow markers show clearly the boundary of the park and the Grouse Nest private property beyond. A walk northward is possible on the Galloping Goose Regional Trail.

Returning to the barrier, a trail immediately to your left leads to Kellett Point, three beaches, lovely grassy slopes and beautiful views of the Sooke Basin and Olympic Mountains. It is an excellent picnic area. Be sure to listen for and spot the Belted Kingfishers in the area. River otters live here too—look for their scat.

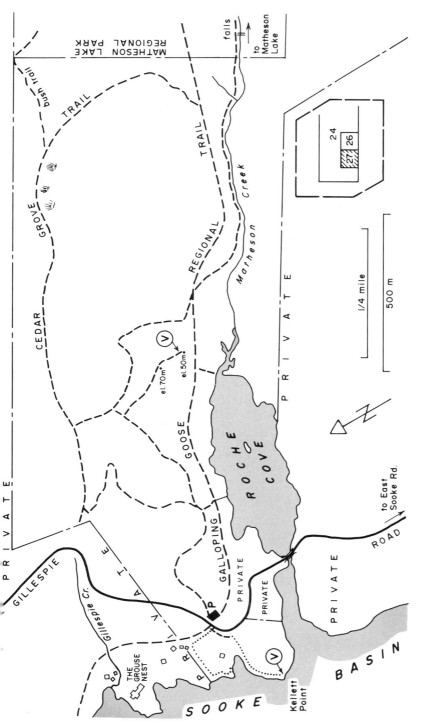

MAP 27: ROCHE COVE REGIONAL PARK

Recross the road into the greater part of Roche Cove Park where you can continue on the Galloping Goose or follow the Matheson Creek Trail into Matheson Lake Park; or explore other trails recently created from older roads. An especially good viewpoint is shown on our map northeast of Roche Cove.

Roche Cove Regional Park was purchased by the CRD in June of 1985. Former Crown Lands designated for park purposes on the north slope of Mt. Matheson were added in the fall of 1989.

The Cove itself is accessible to shallow-draught vessels.

EAST SOOKE REGIONAL PARK (MAP 28)

Access from Victoria is via Highways 1 and 14 and thence either by Gillespie Road and East Sooke Road; or via Metchosin, Rocky Point and East Sooke roads. The distance to Aylard Farm is about 34 km, an hour's drive from Victoria.

There are six access points to the 1422-ha park, but note there are only three parking lots with facilities—at Aylard Farm (gated), Anderson Cove and Pike Road. Families will find hiking from the Aylard Farm end the most rewarding, as there are regular parks facilities, green meadows and good access to sandy beaches, also lookouts at Creyke Point and Beechey Head. Babbington Hill, an excellent viewpoint, is also easily reached from Aylard Farm. The Aylard Farm area and toilets are the only part of the park suitable for wheelchair use.

There is limited parking at access D1 on East Sooke Road. Another access to the same area of the park is off Park Heights Road. Drive to Leda Road and park at the intersection but don't block the narrow extension of Park Heights as it is a fire road and also leads past a private home. Walk the extension of Park Heights for about 350 m to the park entrance which has a locked chain barrier.

The Mount Maguire area may be accessed by taking Copper Mine Road for about 1 km to Valentine Road. Park on the roadside but don't block either road. Walk up Copper Mine Road about 30 m to Gordon Road with a "no exit" sign on the right. Follow Gordon Road about 200 m to the park entrance, which is gated.

This semi-wilderness park, within easy reach of Victoria, is good for year-round hiking offering extensive trails for day hikers. There are many interconnecting trails, all well-cut and signposted. Distances can be deceptive because of the rough terrain so we give here some approximate hiking times. It is wise to start your hike early in the day and not overestimate your capabilities.

In spring and summer, flower enthusiasts may find the following: fringe cup, orange honeysuckle, stonecrop, monkey flower, hardhack, harvest brodiaea, white campion, western buttercup, red columbine, small-flower alumroot, white clover, Queen Anne's lace, Indian paintbrush, seaside woolly sunflower, hedge nettle, clustered

On this map :

— — — moderate trails

·········· rugged trails

⌂   shelter

⚒   mine

SOOKE BAS

D

SEAGIRT RD.

EAST

TIMBERDOODLE RD.

BRECON DR.

Ⓟ

COPPER MINE

S

VALENTINE RD.

FIRE LANE

GORDON RD.

RD.

gate

PARK

Mount
Maguire

el.
272m

Ⓥ

COVE

TRAIL

MINE

ANDERSON

Whiffen

Spit

PIKE RD.

P

gate

⚒

⚒

IRON

SOOKE INLET

Company
Pt.

Iron Mine
Hill

⌂   COAST

TRAIL

O'Brien
Pt.

Iron Mine
Bay

Possession Pt.

Ⓥ

Pike Pt.

Donaldson
(Secretary)
Is.

STRAIT   OF   JUAN   DE   FUCA

MAP 28: EAST SOOKE REGIONAL PARK

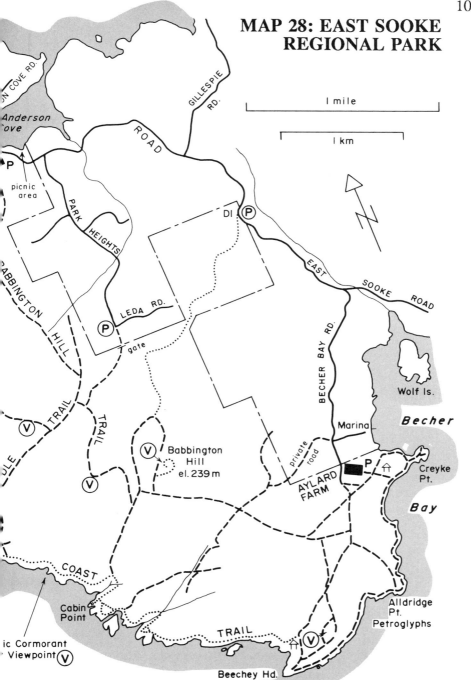

I mile

I km

GILLESPIE RD.

ROAD

Anderson Cove

P

picnic area

PARK HEIGHTS

ROAD

DI

P

LEDA RD.

P

gate

BABBINGTON HILL

EAST

SOOKE ROAD

BECHER BAY RD.

Wolf Is.

Becher

Marina

TRAIL

V

TRAIL

V

Babbington Hill
el. 239 m

V

V

private road

P

AYLARD FARM

Creyke Pt.

Bay

COAST

Cabin Point

Alldridge Pt.
Petroglyphs

ic Cormorant Viewpoint

V

TRAIL

V

Beechey Hd.

wild rose, red elder, mullein, sea blush, Columbia tiger lily, nodding onion and white triteleia.

There is fishing off Beechey Head and at Pike Point. Families of otter living on the rocky beach at Aylard Farm or at Alldridge Point may be seen feeding in the early morning or late evening. You may also see them up and down the Coast Trail. From here seals will be seen frequently and in the summer there can be magnificent viewings of whales. You may see deer at the Aylard Farm end and grouse on the Interior Trail from Babbington Hill onwards.

When hiking in the swampy areas observe the skunk cabbage. In the spring, bears enjoy the centres of skunk cabbages and dandelions. The cougar scratches his territory out like a domestic cat and near the turnoff to Cabin Point there are some alder trees with cougar marks. On the Middle Trail there is quite a raccoon settlement. From the top of Mount Maguire you may see hawks, eagles and pigeons.

For the more energetic hikers the Coast Trail is the best of all. Its scenery is magnificent with good views of the Olympic Peninsula. The coast itself, with deep bays, cliffs and chasms, has an atmosphere of remoteness and adventure. (See our cover photo.)

Iron Mine Bay at the west end of the park has a good pebble beach and some fine views.

There is still evidence of old logging roads throughout the peninsula, but in the main our map shows only the officially signposted trails. If you are new to the park you will be well advised to stay on the marked trails. More than one hiker has unintentionally spent the night in East Sooke Regional Park.

You will find sign boards showing "points of interest". Please do not damage or remove any of these signs.

The Victorienteers (see page 125) have produced a map of the Aylard Farm area; price: $1.00 to non-members for a photo-copy.

Note:
- Do not hike alone. Allow time to get out before nightfall.
- The Aylard Farm parking lot is closed at night.
- Don't rely on creeks for water; always carry your own.
- Carry a map. A CRD Parks brochure is available.

- No camping and no fires are permitted.
- Carry out your own litter.
- The waterfront area near Anderson Cove is a pleasant picnic site.

Approximate hiking times in East Sooke Park:	Hours
Aylard Farm to Pike Road parking lot	6½
Aylard Farm to Beechey Head, via coast	1
Beechey Head to Cabin Point	1½
Cabin Point to Iron Mine Bay	3
Iron Mine Bay to Pike Road parking lot	½
Pike Road parking lot to Anderson Cove, via Anderson Cove Trail	2
Pike Road parking lot to shelter at Iron Mine Bay	½
Pike Road parking lot to Mount Maguire	1
Iron Mine Trail to Interior Trail, from coast	1
Middle Trail to Interior Trail, from coast	½
Anderson Cove Trail to Middle Trail, via Babbington Hill Trail	1¼
Anderson Cove to Babbington Hill	2
Interior Trail, from Anderson Cove Trail to Middle Trail	1¼
Aylard Farm to Babbington Hill	1¼
D1 (at East Sooke Road) to Babbington Hill	1¼

⟨15⟩ SOOKE AREA (MAP 29)

Sooke is a large unincorporated district within the Capital Regional District. It was, for a short time, home to Vancouver Island's first independent settler, Captain Walter Colquhoun Grant, who arrived in Victoria from Scotland in 1849. In 1851 he planted about a dozen seeds of Scottish broom (Cytisus scoparius), which he had received from the British consul during a visit to the Sandwich Islands (Hawaii). He then left the colony for better prospects. His home and land were sold to the Muir family, who spared the three surviving broom bushes because they reminded Mrs. Muir of her Scottish homeland. Broom has spread throughout Vancouver Island and it is getting established on the mainland. Though a thing of beauty when its yellow blooms gild the hillsides in May and June, the plant is too successful in its new habitat. A nitrogen-fixing legume, it builds soil conditions that encourage the spread of orchard grass, another introduced species. Together, the two choke out native species. Where it grows native in the British Isles and Europe, broom is kept under control by natural parasites, insect pests and local conditions. Here, it has no enemies and flourishes in its adopted environment.

The YM-YWCA has developed some good bush trails around **Camp Thunderbird**, all signposted. You may hike there from mid-October to mid-April, but must obtain permission before doing so; phone 386-7511. The Victorienteers (see page 125) have produced a coloured map, scale 1:10000; price: $5.00 to non-members.

An interesting section of the **Galloping Goose Regional Trail** (see page 76) starts at Veitch Creek (Hutchinson Cove), via Manzer Road just past Glinz Lake Road. Distance from Victoria is about 30 km. The old right-of-way along here seems almost to hang out over the water and it must have been a memorable train ride in bygone days. From Veitch Creek to Sooke Potholes Park is 10 km one way, about a 3-hour hike. It is possible to continue on along the right-of-way as far as Leechtown, but the two high trestles over Charters River and Todd Creek are officially posted as closed to the public until bridge upgrading is completed.

Sooke Potholes Park is a delightful spot for swimming and picnicking and the area round about on both sides of the river is well worth exploring. In 1993 discussions were ongoing for the possible transfer of this provincial park to the CRD.

Harrison Trail (a rough old road) leads up towards the top of Empress Mountain from the Sooke Potholes and the view from the top (673 m) can be grand.

Sooke Mountain Provincial Park has been used as a wilderness recreational area since its creation in 1928. Access is from the end of Harbourview Road, which has at times been gated, along a rough road accessible only to four-by-four vehicles, cyclists and pedestrians. For a full description of the area refer to "More Island Adventures, volume 2" by Richard K. Blier (Orca Books Publishers). In 1993 it is proposed that this provincial park be transferred to the CRD. Recreationists used to camping, motorcycling, four-wheel-driving and hunting are protesting the transfer. For up-dated information contact: BC Parks Public Information Officer (Victoria) 387-4609.

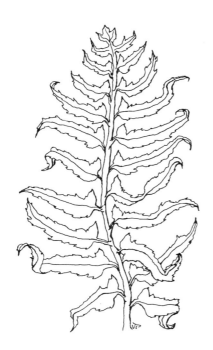

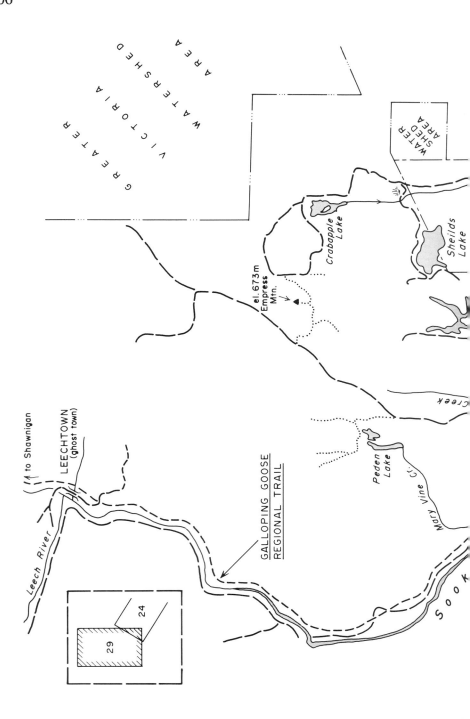

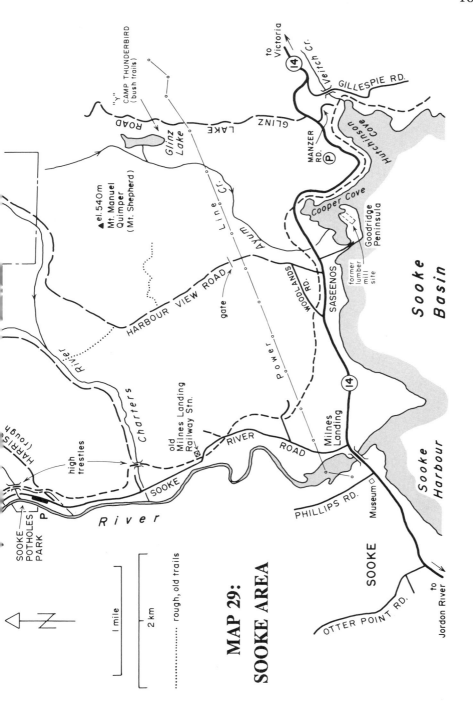

**MAP 29:
SOOKE AREA**

1 mile

2 km

.... rough, old trails

⟨16⟩ BEACH ACCESSES WEST OF SOOKE
(see CONTENTS MAP)

FRENCH BEACH PROVINCIAL PARK
About an hour's drive from Victoria (21.5 km west of Sooke Centre); or 8.2 km west of Muir Creek Bridge. Ample parking. Parks facilities include 69 campsites. Easy trails and a beautiful sandy beach make the day use area wheelchair accessible.

SANDCUT CREEK TRAIL (in WFP Ltd. TFL 25)
From Victoria, 65 km, or from Point No Point Resort 3.7 km to the parking lot. No facilities. A pretty rain forest trail with easy descent leads to a long expanse of sand and pebble beach. Time down— about 10 minutes; up—about 15 minutes. A beach walk from here to Jordan River is about 3 km one way.

JORDAN RIVER RECREATION SITE (WFP Ltd.)
At the mouth of the Jordan River, about 90 minutes' drive from Victoria, (74 km), Western Forest Products Ltd. has provided a parking and picnic area large enough to accommodate campers and trailers, with parks facilities including fire pits and picnic tables.

CHINA BEACH PROVINCIAL PARK
From the Jordan River Bridge it is 4 km to the ample China Beach parking lot. A good trail, fairly steep, but well graded and suitable for family hikers, leads down through rain forest to a long sandy beach. There are toilet facilities but no camping is permitted. Time down— 15 minutes; up—about 25 minutes.

MYSTIC BEACH TRAIL (WFP Ltd., TFL 25)
5.8 km west of the Jordan River Bridge, find the parking area; there are no other facilities. This steep trail (about 1.5 km through rain forest) leads to a lovely sandy beach with interesting rock formations and a waterfall. Time down—about 15 minutes; up—about 25 minutes.

SOMBRIO BEACH TRAILS (WFP Ltd., TFL 25) (MAP 31)
From Victoria it is roughly 90 km, a two-hour drive, to the Sombrio area. Several trails lead down to the beach, with ④ and ⑤ signposted from the highway:

MAP 30: SOMBRIO BEACH TRAILS

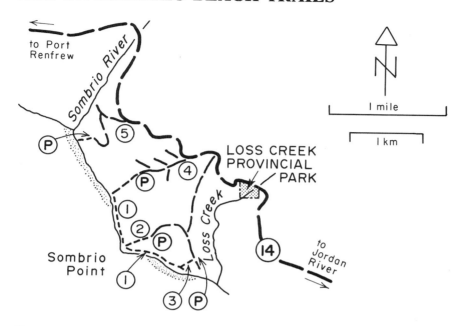

① **Rossalan Trail,** ② **MacInnes Trail,** ③ **Sea Lion Trail:**
In 1976 a group of Outdoor Club of Victoria members, lead by Angie
Rossiter and Alan Warren, started cutting a trail from the south end of
Sombrio Beach east toward Loss Creek. The crew dwindled to the
two leaders, but eventually their goal was accomplished: a seaside
"Rossalan Trail" along this very rugged stretch of coast. The Loss
Creek end of the trail was eventually abandoned, but another new
trail, the "MacInnes Trail", was started in 1978 by Outdoor Club
members Mac Page and Innes Cooper. The MacInnes and Sea Lion
trails made loop hikes possible. Access is via the first logging road to
your left after **Loss Creek Provincial Park. Caution:** these rough,
often over-grown trails lead you into remote, rugged areas. Never
include children or pets in your party: there are dangerous drop-offs
to the ocean. Be prepared to be safe and self-sufficient. And, while
you are there, why not pack along a few tools and leave the trail just a
little better than the way you found it?

④ **Sombrio East Trail:**
23 km west of Jordan River on Highway 14 turn left at the sign onto a
logging spur road and drive straight ahead for about 1 km to a parking
area. The trail from here is steep and currently rough. Some sections

can be muddy during the wet season. Time down to beach—about 15 minutes; up—about 25 minutes. Upon arriving at the beach, head to the right and watch for a stream emerging from the forest. If you follow the stream up from the beach you will be rewarded with the sight of a high, narrow waterfall in a misty grotto.

⑤ **Sombrio West Trail**:
On Highway 14 after a further km westward, turn left at the sign onto a logging spur road. After 1 km turn sharply left again and continue to parking area. From here there is an easy five-minute walk to a beautiful, sandy and rocky beach, typical of Vancouver Island's west coast.

A brochure **"Visitor's Guide to Jordan River Area"** with information on this whole area is available from **Western Forest Products Ltd.** Jordan River Forest Operation, River Jordan, BC V0S 1L0 (phone 646-2031); or in person at their Jordan River office, 8 am–4:30 pm weekdays.

⟨17⟩ PORT RENFREW AREA (MAP 31)

Port Renfrew is located on the west coast of southern Vancouver Island. Access is by one of two routes. From Victoria via Sooke and Jordan River along Highway 14 (the West Coast Road) is about 110 km on a paved road—about 2 hours' driving time; the alternative is to drive in from Cowichan Lake on mostly gravel roads.

HIKING THROUGH HISTORY

"Hiking Through History in Port Renfrew" is the intriguing title of a new booklet being produced by the Port Renfrew Community Association. Eleven trails, varying in length from 0.5 to 6 km, will take you to river sandbars, a waterfall, lakes, a grove of ancient trees and an old railway logging camp. The history of logging in the San Juan Valley is featured in visits to an old timber road, a plank road and a railway grade. The booklet, containing maps, trail information, historical photographs and stories, will be available at a low price from local outlets such as the Port Renfrew Recreation Centre. For further information please contact the Port Renfrew Community Association, General Delivery, Port Renfrew, BC V0S 1K0.

THE RED CREEK TREE

If you are in the Port Renfrew area, don't miss out on the opportunity to visit Canada's largest known Douglas-fir tree. To find it, start at the junction of West Coast Road and the road that crosses the San Juan River, near the townsite. Head back toward Victoria for 2.4 km and turn left onto the Red Creek Mainline. Follow the mainline for 14.5 km to a small parking area. The signposted trail leads you up to the big tree past the Three Guardsmen, three large western red cedars. For information on this and other remarkable trees, consult Randy Stoltmann's "Hiking Guide to the Big Trees of Southwestern British Columbia", published by the Western Canada Wilderness Committee.

SAN JUAN RIDGE

In cooperation with Western Forest Products, Pacific Forest Products and Fletcher Challenge, the Kludahk Outdoors Club is developing a San Juan Ridge trail from Leechtown to Botanical Beach, connecting the Galloping Goose and West Coast trails. Sections near Wye Lake and Noyse Lakes have been completed. Kludahk means "home of the elk." For information please contact

The **Kludahk Outdoors Club**
2037 Kaltasin Road, R R 1 Sooke, BC V0S 1N0
phone 642-3523 (Maywell Wickheim)
642-4342 (Phoebe Dunbar—after 6)

BOTANICAL BEACH PROVINCIAL PARK (MAP 31)

Access to Port Renfrew as above. Just before reaching the Port Renfrew Hotel and government wharf, turn left on Cerantes Road (a small, rough gravel road). Follow the road by vehicle as far as possible, then walk about 45 minutes to the park. High-clearance vehicles may be able to get within 15 minutes' walking time of the beach.

The unique beach area, with tidal pools filled with a variety of marine life, is of particular interest to marine biologists and other naturalists. Dr. Josephine Tildon chose it as the site of the University of Minnesota's marine station in 1900. Access at that time was by steamship from Victoria to Port Renfrew, then on foot along a muddy track.

MAP 31:
BOTANICAL BEACH, PORT RENFREW

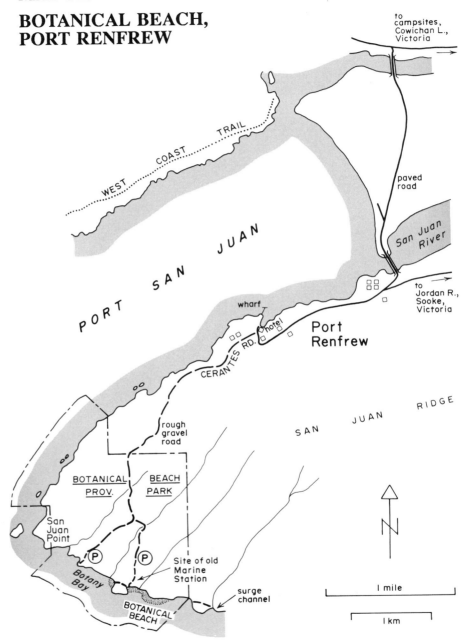

to campsites, Cowichan L., Victoria

WEST COAST TRAIL

paved road

San Juan River

PORT SAN JUAN

wharf

to Jordan R., Sooke, Victoria

hotel

CERANTES RD.

Port Renfrew

SAN JUAN RIDGE

rough gravel road

BOTANICAL PROV.

BEACH PARK

San Juan Point

P

P

Site of old Marine Station

Botany Bay

surge channel

BOTANICAL BEACH

N

1 mile

1 km

This difficult access was a contributing factor in the station's closure in 1907. The Nature Conservancy of Canada has purchased two ha at the original site of the marine station; this is now part of the park. Since the area became a provincial park in 1989, universities still use the beach for research, but under a Park-Use permit.

PLEASE NOTE: NO COLLECTING OR HARMING OF ANY MARINE SPECIES (whether it is alive or not).

Since a very low (1.2-metre or 4-foot) tide is most desirable for viewing tidepools, check tide tables when planning your visit. Obtain "Pacific Coast Tide and Current Tables" Volume 6 and refer to tides at Tofino, using correction for Port Renfrew. This booklet is available from marine chandlers or on loan at local public libraries.

Before visiting Botanical Beach you should read the BC Parks brochure detailing access and the human and natural history of the park. It is available from the Port Renfrew Information Centre or from BC Parks Malahat District office (see page 126). In case you should visit the park without a brochure, we repeat these important BC Parks messages:

- You are in a wilderness area, home to black bears and cougars. Leave your pets at home and keep small children close by at all times.

- There are no garbage facilities, so pack out what you pack in. We do not want the bears to become familiar with human garbage.

- We cannot overemphasize the danger posed by the force of the waves. Periodically and unpredictably a very large wave or a series of large waves will hit the beach. These waves can pull an unsuspecting park visitor into the water. NEVER ALLOW CHILDREN TO PLAY NEAR THE SURF.

- We repeat that you are in a wilderness area: be prepared to be self-sufficient. You should be properly equipped with suitable outer-wear and footwear. Normal precautions should be taken with drinking water in backcountry. The shoreline is very rocky and slippery and first aid is not readily available.

- And, finally, let's keep this wilderness area as we find it. Camping and fires are not permitted in the park.

⟨18⟩ WEST COAST TRAIL (MAP 31)

The West Coast Trail is recommended for experienced backpackers only. The southern trailhead is in the Port Renfrew area. A quota system limiting use is in place. Reservations are advised. Registration and Park-Use permits are mandatory. Reservations can be made between March 1st and September 30th and are available **by phone only** at (604) 728-1282. The line is open **7 days a week** between 10 am and 5 pm Pacific Standard Time. Hikers must be at the trailhead no later than **12 noon** on the day they are scheduled to hike. Hiking space will be forfeited if you are late. There are **no refunds** in the event of a cancellation. Currently (1993) reservations cost $25.00 per person (including GST). Visa or Mastercard are accepted.

Only 52 Park-Use permits will be issued per day; 26 for each trailhead. Of these, 40 permits will be offered for advance reservation; the remaining 12 will be issued to hikers on waitlists at each trailhead. Waitlist permits will be issued at no cost, but demand is high and you could face a 2 or 3 day wait (or longer) for your name to come up on the list. Reservations are highly recommended. You must register at the trailhead prior to your hike.

Canadian Parks Partnership (CPP), a nation-wide non-profit organization working to support and enhance Canada's national parks and national historic sites, operates the West Coast Trail reservation system on behalf of the Canadian Parks Service. For the cost of booking a space, hikers receive a guaranteed reservation for the trail, personal trip counselling, a detailed waterproof trail map and the West Coast Trail Preparation Guide. A portion of the fee goes toward trail maintenance. For further information, contact Canadian Parks Partnership, General Delivery, Bamfield, BC V0R 1B0 or Canadian Parks Partnership, 501 Salem Avenue SW, Calgary, AB T3C 2K7; phone (403) 244-6067; fax (403) 244-1842.

West Coast Trail Reservations: (604) 728-1282.

West Coast Trail Information Centres: Pachena Bay (604) 728-3234; Port Renfrew (604) 647-5434. (Note that West Coast Trail Information Centres are open daily from 9 am to 5 pm, May 1 to September 30 only.)

Air Service: Hanna's Air Saltspring (604) 537-9359

Awood Air Ltd. (604) 656-5521

Bus Service: (Schedules vary throughout the year.)

Port Alberni to Bamfield: Western Bus Lines (604) 723-3341.

Port Renfrew to Bamfield: Pacheenaht Band Bus Service (604) 647-5521.

Victoria to Port Renfrew: West Coast Trail–Port Renfrew Connector (604) 361-9080 (reservations required).

Victoria to Bamfield: West Coast Trail Express (604) 380-0580.

Ferry Service:
Some hikers journey from Port Alberni to Bamfield (or vice versa) on the M.V. Lady Rose. Reservations are required from mid-June through mid-September. For rates and information, contact Alberni Marine Transportation, Box 188, Port Alberni, BC V9Y 7M7, (604) 723-8313; fax (604) 723-8314.

Zodiak service across the Gordon River or to Thrasher Cove can be arranged at the Port Renfrew Marina (Norm Smith) (604) 647-5430.

Helpful Books and Maps:

- A special waterproof topographical map of the West Coast Trail (scale 1:50,000) (available from Maps BC) is included in the trail reservation package.

- The Canadian Tide and Current Tables: Volume 6, published by the Canadian Hydrographic Service.

- Guide to the Forestlands of Southern Vancouver Island (1992) compiled by the Lake Cowichan Combined Fire Organization.

- MacMillan Bloedel TFL 44 Recreation and Logging Road Guide (East Map).

- West Coast Trail and Carmanah Pacific Park map (1:50,000) published (1992) by ITMB Publishing Ltd. for World Wide Books.

- **Adventuring in British Columbia (1991)** by Isabel Nanton and Mary Simpson has a section on the West Coast Trail and an account of a trip to Bamfield on the MV Lady Rose.

- **Blisters and Bliss, A Trekkers Guide to the West Coast Trail (revised edition, 1991)** by David Foster and Wayne Aitken, illustrated by Nelson Dewey, is a practical and often humourous guide to the West Coast Trail.

- **Island Adventures, An Outdoors Guide to Vancouver Island (1989)** by Richard K. Blier, details logging road travel to both the Port Renfrew and Pachena Bay trailheads and contains a section on the West Coast Trail. Separate chapters describe canoeing the Nitinat Triangle and Nitinat Lake.

- **More Island Adventures, An Outdoors Guide to Vancouver Island (1993)** by Richard K. Blier, gives an account of an off-season hike from Pachena Bay to Tsusiat Falls.

- **The Pacific Rim Explorer (1986)** by Bruce Obee, includes information on the Nitinat Triangle, the Broken Islands Group, Barkley Sound and the coastal area up to Hot Springs Cove.

- **The West Coast Trail and Nitinat Lakes, (7th revised edition, 1992)** by the Sierra Club of BC has detailed descriptions and maps for the West Coast Trail and canoeing trips to the Nitinat Triangle.

⟨19⟩ MALAHAT AREA

These hills acquired their native name, meaning "caterpillared," after a particularly devastating infestation of tent caterpillars.

Goldstream Provincial Park, situated wholly within the District of Langford boundaries, is presented here because it is the start of the famous Malahat Drive.

GOLDSTREAM PROVINCIAL PARK (MAP 32)

Just over 16 km from Victoria, Highway 1 winds its way through Goldstream Park (327 ha) which rises majestically on either hand. There are many parking areas. An excellent BC Parks brochure is available at the Gate House and the Visitor Centre.

The park's diverse terrain (from rain forest to dry ridges of arbutus and pine) attracts groups of all ages. There are many interconnecting forest trails with viewpoints and points of interest which are marked on our map. The Niagara Falls, viewed from the trail below, are a most spectacular sight, particularly in the spring when they are in full spate. The Freeman King Visitor Centre in the Flats provides informative exhibits; in summer, talks are also arranged for visitors at the Meeting Place in the campground. Parking is limited at the campground. Contact BC Parks Malahat District office at 387-4363 or the Visitor Centre at 478-9414 for more information on programs.

In the late fall crowds gather along the whole stretch of Goldstream River to watch the returning salmon spawn. Please avoid the Upper Goldstream Trail in the Campground area during spawning season. The coho and chinook that spawn in the upper reaches are returning in such low numbers that human intrusion must be avoided. It is critical that pets be kept on leash and under control at all times and that they never enter the water.

The trail from the parking lot to the Visitor Centre, a loop trail along the river, the Visitor Centre itself and the toilets at both the Picnic Area and the Visitor Centre are all wheelchair accessible.

The trails in the park are suitable for hiking year round. Some were constructed by the BC Provincial Parks Branch. The Outdoor Club of Victoria built the Arbutus Ridge, Gold Mine, Prospectors and Riverside Trails, and maintains them with periodic volunteer work parties.

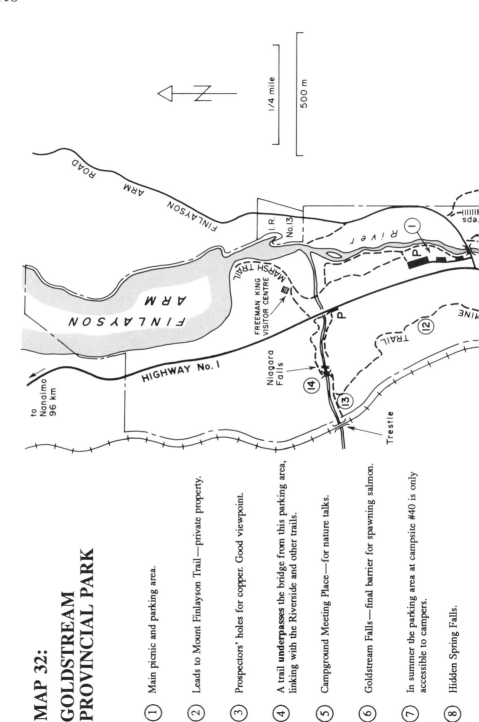

MAP 32:
GOLDSTREAM
PROVINCIAL PARK

1. Main picnic and parking area.

2. Leads to Mount Finlayson Trail—private property.

3. Prospectors' holes for copper. Good viewpoint.

4. A trail **underpasses** the bridge from this parking area, linking with the Riverside and other trails.

5. Campground Meeting Place—for nature talks.

6. Goldstream Falls—final barrier for spawning salmon.

7. In summer the parking area at campsite #40 is only accessible to campers.

8. Hidden Spring Falls.

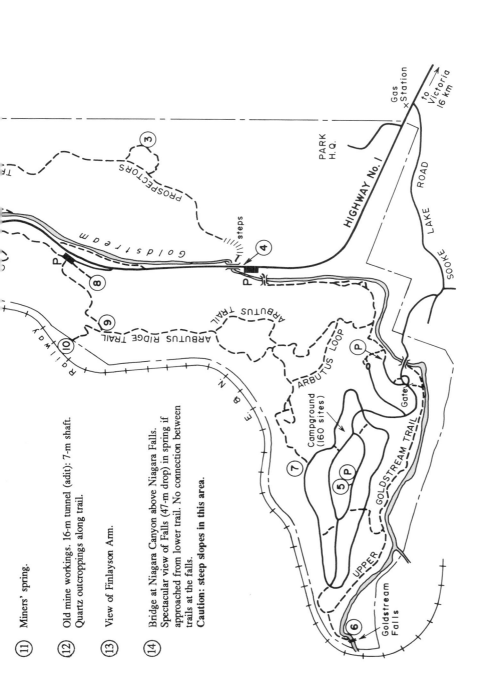

⑪ Miners' spring.

⑫ Old mine workings. 16-m tunnel (adit): 7-m shaft. Quartz outcroppings along trail.

⑬ View of Finlayson Arm.

⑭ Bridge at Niagara Canyon above Niagara Falls. Spectacular view of Falls (47-m drop) in spring if approached from lower trail. No connection between trails at the falls. **Caution: steep slopes in this area.**

An Environment Youth Corp crew, with support from Pacific Coast Savings Credit Union and the Ministry of Environment's Youth Corp program upgraded the Prospectors Trail in 1990. The South Vancouver Island Rangers, a search and rescue group, built the Mount Finlayson Trails. Note that **Mount Finlayson** is outside the park. BC Parks is interested in acquiring this area. **Skirt Mountain**, south of Mount Finlayson, has several mining claims and mine workings. It is not advisable to hike here with small dogs or small children.

Randy Stoltmann's "Hiking Guide to the Big Trees of Southwestern British Columbia" describes a walk in Goldstream Park.

SPECTACLE LAKE PROVINCIAL PARK AND OLIPHANT LAKE (MAP 33)

On Highway 1 travelling north past the first Shawnigan Lake cutoff, continue .8 km then turn left onto Whitaker Road—signposted to Spectacle Lake Park (65 ha). About 1 km more brings you to the parking lot (about 30 km total from Victoria). There are parks facilities for day use; no camping is permitted. It is open year-round, free of charge. The toilets and the trail along the east side of the lake are wheelchair-accessible.

Spectacle Lake (so named as it resembles a pair of spectacles) is a pretty little lake, good for swimming, and a walk around it takes under an hour. It is said to have eastern brook trout in it. It's also one of the best spots near Victoria for open air ice skating in winter.

A good hike is possible from here to Oliphant Lake which is harder to find, as for the most part it is not visible from its eastern side. Follow the trail on the east side of Spectacle Lake and continue north on a pleasant woodsy trail ① ascending gradually for about 30 minutes to a T junction ②.

About a 10-minute hike to your left will bring you to a rough road. A right or left turn will lead you to the trails around Oliphant Lake. There is access to three good swimming and camping spots as shown on our map. At the north arm of the lake ③ a horse trail continues north, then west, and then veers north-east crossing the power line nearly 2 km north of Johns Creek. Just south of the creek at ④ there is an excellent view of the Saanich Inlet. Other pleasant views can be found by picking your own route up to the open areas shown. Mount Wood is the highest point of the Malahat Ridge.

MAP 33:
SPECTACLE LAKE PROVINCIAL PARK, OLIPHANT LAKE

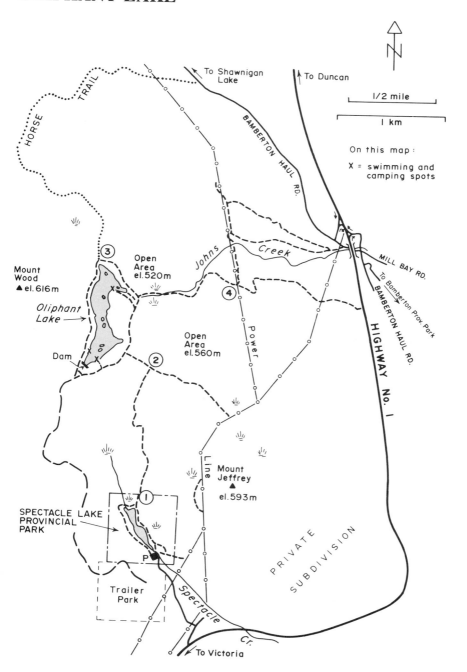

If returning via the powerline, you might miss the trail leading back to the T junction ②, but the power line will lead you back to the Spectacle Lake parking lot. Crossing the creek is sometimes difficult, but there is a little trail to the right leading to the main trail.

The route via ① ② ③ ② ① with a side trip to the viewpoint at the north end of the lake takes about four hours.

A rough road (4-wheel drive vehicles only) leads south from Oliphant Lake back to Spectacle Lake via the trailer park.

The rare Mountain Quail may be seen along the power line. In summer, wild strawberries are a treat.

This is the only destination in this book that is outside the Capital Regional District. The **Cowichan Valley Regional District**, with cooperation from BC Hydro, is planning trail expansion in this area, including a trail to the summit of Mount Jeffrey. For information please contact the CVRD Planning Department (see page 126).

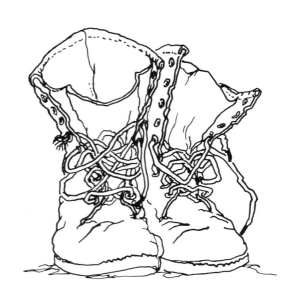

TRAIL SYSTEMS

CAPITAL REGIONAL DISTRICT (CRD) REGIONAL TRUNK TRAIL SYSTEM

Imagine a continuous trail from the tip of the Saanich Peninsula all the way to the start of the West Coast Trail near Port Renfrew— others have, and many of them serve as members of the Regional Trails Coordinating Group (RTCG), a body that addresses matters dealing with planning, acquiring land, and developing just such a trail. The RTCG advises the CRD and local municipalities on how best to link up major parks and sites of scenic and historical interest along local trails. Many of the trails described in this book are part of this Regional Trail system including, most obviously, the Galloping Goose Regional Trail.

VICTORIA–COWICHAN TRAIL

The Transportation and Highways Ministry has plans for leasing agreements that would allow the Capital Regional District (CRD) and the Cowichan Valley Regional District (CVRD) to convert sections of the abandoned CNR line into a recreational corridor to extend from the present end of the Galloping Goose Regional Trail at Leechtown all the way to Lake Cowichan. This part of the route is as yet undeveloped and is not enthusiastically recommended. Heading north from Leechtown, the right-of-way becomes overgrown or blocked and may be difficult to follow around missing trestles. However, hikers, bikers or horseback riders, if they wish to make the effort, can follow the adjacent gravel highway 117 which follows the shore of Sooke Lake to Shawnigan Lake. For vehicles to complete a through trip from Sooke to Shawnigan Lake via Boneyard Main and highway 117 involves fording the river at Leechtown. **Special note:** On the approximately 13 km of this road within the Greater Victoria Water District one is required to stay **on** the road at **all** times. The route is scenic but is not one of the more pleasant hikes, particularly when the road is dry and dusty. Carry water; leave nothing along the roadside; do not leave the road. This is in the interests of water quality and fire risk and there are **no** exceptions. From the west side of Shawnigan Lake the route continues north to Deerholme, where a spur runs east to Duncan. This 25.7-km stretch includes the Kinsol trestle over the Koksilah River. From Deerholme west the route roughly follows the Cowichan River for 22.5 km.

VANCOUVER ISLAND BACKBONE TRAIL

The goal of the Mid-Island Branch of the Western Canada Wilderness Committee is a continuous north-south hiking route for Vancouver Island. Mapping is underway in summer 1993 to link the areas near Sooke, Cowichan Lake, Nanaimo Lakes, Port Alberni, Comox Lake, Tahsis, Woss Lake and on to Port McNeill. Much of the route retraces the steps of William Washington Bolton who in 1894 was the first white explorer to travel the north/south route. The Grand Opening is scheduled to coincide with the Commonwealth Games in Victoria in 1994. For information please contact:

> Mid-Island Branch, **Western Canada Wilderness Committee**
> Box 1153, Station A, Nanaimo, BC V9R 6E7
> phone (604) 756-0084; fax (604) 756-9433

CENTENNIAL TRAILS TRUST

The CTT is a non-profit provincial organization responsible for the development and management of a hiking trail across BC from Victoria to Banff, Alberta. Starting in Victoria, the trail would follow the Galloping Goose Regional Trail to Leechtown, then the Lake Cowichan route described above. Trails or logging roads would complete the route to Nanaimo and the ferry to Horseshoe Bay. On the West Vancouver side the proposal links up many existing trails, including the Centennial Trail and the Dewdney Heritage Trail. For information please contact:

> The **Centennial Trails Trust**
> #203-1646 West 7th Ave., Vancouver, BC V6J 1S5

TRANS CANADA TRAIL / SENTIER TRANSCANADIEN

Once into Alberta, the trail described above links with the National Trail of Canada, and could take you coast-to-coast, all the way from Victoria, BC to St. John's, Newfoundland. A north-south spur will run from Calgary through the Yukon to Tuktoyaktuk, NWT. Plans are to have a 15,000-km trail for hikers, equestrians, skiers and non-motorized vehicles (with snowmobiles where desired) in place by the year 2000. Funding is to come from corporate and private sponsors ($36 buys you a metre of trail); amenities are to include toilets, campsites and hostels. For information please contact:

> **Trans Canada Trail Foundation**
> 837 Second Ave. S W, Calgary, AB T2P 0E6
> phone (403) 731-9195 or 1-800-465-3636

CLUB ADDRESSES

Many hiking groups welcome non-members on scheduled outings. Any hiking group wishing to have its name appear in future revisions of this book should contact:

Vancouver Island Trails Information Society
c/o Sono Nis Press, 1745 Blanshard St.
Victoria, BC V8W 2J8

Outdoor Club of Victoria:
The OCV was formed in 1942 by a group of Victorians interested in hiking together so they could share the companionship of others with similar interests and pool their knowledge of places to go. There are hikes every Saturday and Sunday throughout the year and monthly evening meetings with entertainment programs. The current issue of the hiking schedule (The Groundsheet) with telephone numbers as to who to contact is available at the Greater Victoria Public Library (see page 126).

Alpine Club of Canada, Vancouver Island section: contact the Greater Victoria Public Library.

Club Tread: contact the Greater Victoria Public Library.

Island Mountain Ramblers
PO Box 691, Nanaimo, BC V9R 5M2

The **Alpine Club** and the **Ramblers** have district representatives.

The **Federation of Mountain Clubs of British Columbia** has information on other hiking clubs on Vancouver Island:
336-1367 West Broadway, Vancouver, BC V6H 4A9
phone (604) 737-3053.

Victorienteers Orienteering Club

Mail to:	Maps from: Alan Philip
504-620 View Street	1608 Ash Road
Victoria, BC V8W 1J6	Victoria, BC V8N 2T1
phone (604) 380-6562	phone (604) 721-5759

USEFUL ADDRESSES

BC Parks, Malahat District
2930 Trans-Canada Highway
R R 6 Victoria, BC V9B 5T9
phone (604) 387-4363

Capital Regional District
Parks Division
490 Atkins Road
Victoria, BC V9B 2Z8
phone (604) 474-3344; fax (604) 478-5416
24-hr recorded message: (604) 474-7275

Cowichan Valley Regional District
137 Evans Street
Duncan, BC V9L 1P5
phone (604) 746-2500

Greater Victoria Public Library
735 Broughton Street
Victoria, BC V8W 3H2
phone (604) 382-7241; fax (604) 382-7125

ACKNOWLEDGEMENTS

In addition to the original contributors, we are indebted to the following individuals and groups who have assisted with this revision:

BC Parks, Malahat District (Debby Funk, Don McLaren, Bob Austad, Derrick Auringer)

CRD Parks (Trish Bland, Christine Morissette)

Municipal staff in North Saanich, Sidney, Central Saanich, Saanich, Oak Bay, Victoria, Esquimalt, View Royal, Langford, Colwood and Metchosin

Richard K. Blier
Josephine Doman
Edo Nyland
Dunsmuir Lodge
Victorienteers (Carl Coger)
The Gowlland Foundation (Nancy McMinn)
Friends of Mount Douglas Park
Thetis Park Nature Sanctuary Association
Western Forest Products Ltd., Jordan River
Angie Rossiter
Port Renfrew Community Association (Theresa Burton)
Garry Oak Meadow Preservation Society (Joyce Lee)
Friends of Knockan Hill Park
Friends of John Dean Park (Dr. Dieter Weichert)
Dr. Thom Hess
BC Transit
Kludahk Outdoors Club (Phoebe Dunbar)

Arnold Fraser, for his patience and precision

Morriss Printing, for their advice and expertise.

INDEX

NOTE: **Bold print** indicates a map reference.

130

APPENDIX

HIKING TRAILS—How to Get There by Public Transit

Swartz Bay Ferry Terminal	70 Pat Bay Hwy
Resthaven Park	70 Pat Bay Hwy
Reay Creek Park	70 Pat Bay Hwy
Sidney Island Ferry	70 Pat Bay Hwy
Coles Bay Regional Park	70 Pat Bay Hwy
John Dean Park	70 Pat Bay Hwy and short walk
Dunsmuir Lodge	70 Pat Bay Hwy
Centennial Park	75 Central Saanich
Island View Beach	70 Pat Bay Hwy then walk
Logan Park	21 Interurban
Elk/Beaver Lake Regional Park	70 Pat Bay Hwy
Cordova Bay Park	31 Glanford to 32 Cordova Bay
Lochside Park	32 Cordova Bay
Mount Douglas Park	28 Majestic
Braefoot Park	20 Cook
Beckwith Park	6 Quadra
Cedar Hill Golf Course	20 Cook
Cedar Hill Recreation Centre	20 Cook
Swan Lake/Christmas Hill Nature Sanctuary	70 Pat Bay Hwy/75 Central Saanich
Quick's Bottom	21 Interurban
Copley Park	30 Carey
Hyacinth Park	21 Interurban
Tillicum Mall	10 Gorge/21 Interurban/22 Burnside
Cuthbert Holmes Park	10 Gorge
Knockan Hill Park	22 Burnside
Gorge Waterway Park	10 Gorge
University of Victoria	14 University
Mount Tolmie	4 Mt. Tolmie
Henderson Recreation Centre	14 University
Uplands Park	11 Uplands
Willows Park	1 Willows
Oak Bay Marina	2 Oak Bay
Oak Bay Recreation Centre	11 Uplands

Pemberton Park	1 Richardson/Willows
Oak Bay Village	1 Richardson/2 Oak Bay
Windsor Park	2 Oak Bay/Gonzales
Gonzales Hill Regional Park	2 Gonzales
Walbran Park	1 Richardson
Summit Park	20 Cook
Ross Bay Cemetery	2 Oak Bay/Gonzales
Beacon Hill Park	5 Fairfield/Beacon Hill
Odgen Point breakwater	30 Carey/31 Glanford
Johnson Street Bridge	23 Esquimalt
Barnard Park	23 Esquimalt/25 Munro
Saxe Point Park	24 Colville/25 Munro
Fleming Beach	25 Munro
HighrockCairn Park	24 Colville
Kinsmen Gorge Park	10 Gorge
West Bay Walkway	24 Colville/25 Munro
Portage Park	14 Craigflower
View Royal Park	14 Craigflower
Parson's Bridge	50 Goldstream
Thetis Lake Park	50 Goldstream
Goldstream Provincial Park	50 Goldstream to 57 Humpback
Mill Hill Regional Park	50 Goldstream
Juan de Fuca Recreation Centre	50 Goldstream
Fort Rodd Hill	50 Goldstream-short walk
Esquimalt Lagoon	50 Goldstream
Hatley Park	50 Goldstream/52 Wishart/61 Sooke
Canwest Mall	50 Goldstream
Seabluff Trail	50 Goldstream to 54 Metchosin
Devonian Park	50 Goldstream to 54 Metchosin
Metchosin Wilderness Park	50 Goldstream to 54 Metchosin
Witty's Lagoon Regional Park	50 Goldstream to 54 Metchosin
Roche Cove Regional Park	61 Sooke
East Sooke Regional Park	61 Sooke
Town of Sooke	61 Sooke

**For more information and schedules please call
BUSLINE at 382-6161.**